THE VEGAN BAKED DONUT COOKBOOK

THE VEGAN BAKED DONUT COOKBOOK

Ally Lazare

50 Recipes to Satisfy Your Cravings

ROCKRIDGE
PRESS

Interior and Cover Designer: Amanda Kirk
Art Producer: Samantha Ulban
Editor: Anne Goldberg
Production Editor: Rachel Taenzler
Production Manager: Riley Hoffman

Photography © 2022 Hélène Dujardin. Food styling by Lisa Rovick.

Paperback ISBN: 978-1-63807-783-1
eBook ISBN: 978-1-63878-909-3
R0

For Audrey and Autumn—the sweetest
inspiration in the world.
Donut forget how much I love you.
And always, for Aaron—who makes
this dream possible.

CONTENTS

Introduction viii

CHAPTER 1
The Vegan Donuts of Your Dreams
1

CHAPTER 2
Plain and Sugared Donuts
25

CHAPTER 3
Glazed and Frosted Donuts
47

CHAPTER 4
Filled Donuts
75

CHAPTER 5
Savory Donuts
101

CHAPTER 6
Not Quite Donuts
115

Measurement Conversions 135

Resources 136

Index 138

INTRODUCTION

ELCOME TO *THE VEGAN BAKED DONUT COOKBOOK!* I'm so excited to show you the world of delicious baked vegan donuts that are easy to make at home and enjoy whenever the craving strikes. Donuts have made a huge comeback in recent years, becoming covetable gourmet treats and not just something you grab with your morning coffee. Many dedicated donut shops pride themselves on creating decadent, over-the-top donut flavors, elevating them to superstar status.

However, if you're vegan, or avoiding dairy and eggs because of allergies, finding suitable donut options can be tricky. When my family and I adopted a vegan diet a decade ago, finding dairy-and-egg-free treats, particularly baked goods, was next to impossible, even though we live in a large metropolitan city with huge culinary diversity. It was years before we found a bakery that made vegan donuts, and even so, the flavor selection was limited. And while vegan donut shops do exist, and some mainstream donut shops are beginning to add vegan options to their menus, they are often few and far between, making them inconvenient for satisfying a quick craving—or the donuts are made with too much oil and sugar.

So I took matters into my own hands (literally) and began making vegan donuts at home. And now I'm sharing them with you. In this book I'll share recipes, tips, and tricks for turning indulgent, once-in-a-while treats into healthy-ish desserts you can make in your own kitchen any time.

I'll show you how easy it is to make both cake and yeasted donuts in a wide variety of flavors and styles, like glazed, sugared, stuffed, and even savory donuts. I've designed the recipes in this book to be easy and delicious, so even if you've never made a donut before, you'll be able to do this. We'll explore a variety of ways to sweeten donuts without always relying on refined sugar and adapt recipes to address specific dietary considerations and allergies by avoiding ingredients like gluten or nuts. There's even a chapter with recipes for donut-like treats such as fritters, éclairs, donut holes, and more.

Every recipe in this book can be made using standard or mini donut pans and cutters, and many have been adapted for use with a mini donut machine as well. Throughout the book, I'll share tips and techniques to elevate your baked donuts and offer ways to switch up or vary a recipe for a special occasion.

I'm excited to bake with you—so let's get started!

**Cherry-Glazed
D'oh! Nuts, page 58**

CHAPTER 1

THE VEGAN DONUTS OF YOUR DREAMS

Before we start baking, let's go through the basics of making vegan donuts at home. In this introductory chapter, we'll set you up for success as a vegan donut maker by exploring the best ways to prep ingredients and workspaces, talking about ingredient substitutions and equipment, and troubleshooting common issues so that you're ready to tackle any recipe in this book. We'll look at all the must-have tools for your kitchen, break down the difference between cake and yeasted (or raised) donuts, explain how to master working with yeast, and dispel the myth that vegan baking is overly complicated and troublesome.

DONUT WORRY ABOUT IT—VEGAN BAKING MADE EASY

How many times have you heard the saying "Cooking is an art, but baking is a science"? Or how many times have you said, "I can't bake. It's too technical for me"? I'm here to help you change that.

It's true that baking is more exacting than cooking, and you do need to pay more attention to what ingredients you use, what order you use them in, and how you measure them. But once you learn those skills, baking can be an enjoyable (and delicious) experience.

Vegan baking often gets a bad rap because many common ingredients are off the table (looking at you there, milk, butter, and eggs) and require work-arounds. Fortunately, many bakers before you have done all kinds of legwork and figured out the best plant-based substitutes for dairy and egg products and how to make them work in vegan baking. We're also lucky to be living in a time when so many plant-based alternatives to traditional dairy, meat, and egg products exist, which makes swapping out ingredients even easier. At one time, veganizing a baking recipe would have been intimidating because of ingredients like milk, butter, or even cream cheese. Now all we need to do is wander down the aisles of almost any mainstream grocery store to find the plant-based alternatives to these products and use them in the same amounts as their dairy-based counterparts.

In general, baked donut recipes are less complicated than pastries or other desserts, so overall the techniques we use will be simpler as well. The only exception to this is working with yeast, which needs time to bloom and to proof. I won't lie—yeast can be a little fussy, but it's nothing to be scared of. We'll get into the specifics of baking with yeast later in this chapter, but really, it comes down to allowing it time and space to do its work so you can do yours, which is making delicious donuts.

So even if you've never made a donut before, or you haven't done much baking in general, this book will guide you on how to expertly stock your kitchen, choose the best tools, and use easy-to-follow recipes to create donuts that look like they came from a fancy donut shop.

Most of the donut recipes in this book are for cake-based donuts, which means they use similar ingredients to cakes and cupcakes and are baked in the oven the same way, just using a special pan (or are made in a mini donut machine). Cake donuts use traditional leaveners like baking soda and baking powder and have a spongy, cake-like consistency to them. And because they are baked, they don't require extra time for chilling or setting up, like fried donuts do. About a dozen recipes in this book are for yeast-based donuts. For the most part, I've limited yeast donuts to the stuffed donut chapters, because donuts made with yeast typically rise more than cake-based ones and have airy, fluffy layers that work well for filling with creams or jams.

KNOW YOUR DONUT

Typically, when we think of donuts, we imagine a round fried disc of sweetened cake or yeast dough with a hole in the middle, like the kind you would find at any donut shop. For a long time, this has been the standard for donut shops, but it's not always ideal for making donuts at home. While fried sweet dough is delicious with its typically crispier shell and soft inside, it's messy to make and not as healthy, because it's deep-fried. If you're baking donuts at home with any sort of regularity, fried donuts are something you'd want to avoid not only because of how complicated they are to make but also because ingesting all that oil isn't the healthiest option.

We're going to explore the world of baked donuts in this book. Baked donuts generally fall into two categories: those made with yeast and those made with cake batter.

Let Them Eat Cake

Most of the recipes in the following pages are for cake donuts, which means they are essentially made from the same batter you would use to make cakes, cupcakes, or muffins. Cake donuts can absolutely be fried, but they are also easy to prepare by baking them in special baking pans with donut-shaped cavities or in a mini donut machine. Cake donuts (much like cake itself) are well suited to different flavors, because the batter is so customizable. Most chocolate donuts (whether fried or baked) are cake donuts.

The main difference between cake and yeast donuts is that cake-based donuts use baking powder and/or baking soda as leaveners, again much like a traditional cake, whereas yeast donuts rely on, well, yeast to make them rise. Cake donuts have a moist, crumbly, or sometimes fluffy inside, like cake or muffins. They are easy to make, don't require any special preparation techniques or proofing/chilling time, and are well suited to home bakers or those who want the instant gratification of making and eating their donuts rather quickly.

Getting a Rise Out of Yeast

A yeast donut is made with dough that's leavened with yeast, just like bread. Yeast donuts are typically cut with a donut or biscuit cutter and baked on a flat baking sheet (or fried in oil, but that's another book!). Yeast donuts are light and airy on the inside and have a good chew to them. Because yeast donuts are much lighter and softer than their cake-based counterparts, you'll typically find these donuts topped with a thin glaze or light icing rather than full frosting and tons of toppings. (Cake-based donuts have a sturdier structure that can handle more toppings and heavier frostings.)

Yeast-based donuts tend to be more mildly flavored and have a slightly tangy, yeasty overtone to their taste. They also use less flour and butter to make, so they aren't typically as rich as cake donuts. If you're a jelly donut fan, then you're going to want to be on Team Yeast, as the air pockets that form when yeast donuts are cooked are what make room for your favorite cream or jelly filling inside. Overall, baked yeast donuts take much longer to make, because the dough needs to proof for an extended amount of time, then bake for a longer amount of time, too.

PREP LIKE A PRO

Nothing is more frustrating than starting a bake and realizing that you don't have easy access to all the tools you need, or you need to stop what you're doing to search for an ingredient. These are a few simple strategies that I use in my kitchen and that you can use to ensure your baking runs smoothly every time:

Take stock: Plan your baking around your grocery shopping routine. Check your pantry and refrigerator to see whether you're missing any ingredients (or if any have expired and need replacing) and pick them up on your next shopping trip.

Mise en place: "Mise en place" is a French culinary term that means "everything in its place." Cooks and bakers use a mise en place strategy to make sure

they have everything they need within arm's reach before starting to cook or bake—like ingredients, cutting boards, mixing bowls, and other tools.

Dedicated pantry space: I like to keep all my baking ingredients on a dedicated shelf in my pantry so that I can easily access them when it's time to bake. It also lets me see what I'm running low on and need to replace on my next grocery trip.

Organized workspace: Aside from having everything in its place, it's also important to ensure you have a "place for everything." Baking often requires ample counter space (especially if you're working with yeast donuts that need a place to proof), so it's a good idea to clear a dedicated workspace in your kitchen so you're not bumping into things (or spilling them) while you're baking.

Mastering Measurements

If you're used to cooking rather than baking, you likely know that it's okay to be a little "free and easy" when it comes to measuring. After all, most recipes that have been handed down from generation to generation have always started with "a pinch of this and a dash of that."

We've come a long way since then in terms of standardizing measurements, and that's never been more important than when baking. Adding too much liquid to a savory dish, like a sauce, can easily be corrected by adding a thickener like cornstarch or flour, and dishes that are too dry can always be fixed with a little bit of broth or water.

But baking is a different story. Because baking requires the use of science and the balance of chemical compounds like acids and bases (think baking soda and vinegar) to achieve the intended results, the amount you use of each ingredient—and in some cases, the order you add those ingredients—makes a huge difference in the outcome of the dish. Baked goods require the right balance of dry and wet ingredients and a constant (often low) heat to bake properly. For example, if the proportion of wet ingredients in a cake donut batter were too high, the donut would sink from the weight. Trying to get it to bake right through to the center would mean the outside would burn or dry out before the middle was set. Conversely, too large a share of dry ingredients will make your donuts dry and crumbly and will prevent them from holding their shape.

DRY INGREDIENTS

Measuring dry ingredients accurately is critical to ensuring your donuts bake properly. There are two standard methods for measuring dry ingredients: by volume (cups) and by weight (grams). To measure dry ingredients by volume, you need to have dry measures, meaning a set of nesting measuring cups and spoons. Typically, ingredients like flour, sugar, baking soda, baking powder, and salt are measured using dry measures, along with solid or semisolid items like peanut butter, yogurt, solid coconut oil, chocolate chips, or nuts.

To accurately measure dry ingredients (like flour) **by volume**, you should place your measuring cup over a canister, sink, or tray that can catch any spillover. Lightly spoon the flour into the cup using a regular tablespoon until the cup is overflowing. Be careful not to pack the flour down into the cup. Take a knife or spatula and slide the back of it over the top rim of the cup to level out the flour, then transfer it to your mixing bowl or stand mixer.

This method also applies to baking powder and baking soda, although with those ingredients, a measuring spoon would be used to scoop the ingredient before leveling off with a knife or spatula.

When it comes to sugar, granulated and powdered (or confectioners') sugars are measured the same way. Brown sugar, however, works a little differently depending on whether the recipe calls for firmly or loosely packed. Loosely packed brown sugar would be measured the same way as granulated, whereas firmly packed requires you to stuff as much sugar in the measuring cup as possible by packing it down with the spoon or your fingers after each addition.

Measuring by weight (using a kitchen scale) is the most accurate way to measure ingredients, because weight is consistent regardless of volume—or of the state of the ingredient (melted, chopped, packed). To measure **by weight**, use a standard kitchen scale and place your mixing bowl on top of it, then hit the "zero" or "tare" button. This resets the scale back to zero after accounting for the weight of your bowl. Now you're ready to add your ingredient to the bowl by the spoonful until you reach the desired weight.

WET INGREDIENTS

Measuring liquids (or wet ingredients) requires two simple things: a level counter space and a glass measuring cup. To measure anything that you need ¼ cup or more of, use a transparent glass or plastic measuring cup and place it on a flat surface, like your counter. Crouch down so that you are eye level with the markings on the glass before you start pouring and then pour until you reach the desired amount. (Any liquid less than ¼ cup can be measured using a standard set of measuring spoons.)

Never hold a measuring glass in your hand in the air or pour while looking down at the glass, because your pour won't be level and the amount of the ingredient you're using won't be accurate.

If you're measuring anything that requires less than ¼ cup of liquid, use a standard measuring spoon. Hold it over the sink, not the mixing bowl, and pour until the liquid reaches the brim. (Pro tip: Holding your spoon over the sink ensures that if any extra spills out, it doesn't land in your bowl and interfere with the amount required by the recipe.)

VOLUME VERSUS WEIGHT

The standard for most cookbooks, particularly here in the United States, is to measure dry ingredients by volume, which is why you'll see ingredients listed in cups or spoons in most books. Measuring dry ingredients by volume, particularly in baking, isn't the most accurate method, however, which is why in this book I've measured large volumes of dry ingredients (like flour, sugar, or cocoa powder) by weight and included the volume equivalent. Anything requiring less than ¼ cup (by volume) I've listed just by volume only, as the amounts are small enough that they won't significantly affect your recipe's outcome.

ESSENTIAL EQUIPMENT

Believe it or not, you don't need a bunch of fancy tools or equipment to make delicious baked donuts at home. In fact, most of what you'll need is likely already in your kitchen. There are a few handy tools that will make the process easier, though, and I've compiled a list of the best "must-have" tools and equipment to make your donut baking a success.

Mixing bowls: A set of three or four nesting mixing bowls, preferably with nonskid bottoms, is ideal for mixing batters and fillings.

Standardized measuring cups and spoons: One set of measuring cups for dry measures and, if budget and space allow, two sets of measuring spoons so that you can keep wet and dry ingredients separate.

4-cup glass measuring cup: Glass measuring cups come in 1-, 2-, and 4-cup sizes. A 4-cup measure is easiest to have on hand if your kitchen storage space is limited.

Silicone spatulas and whisks: A standard set of spatulas and a large balloon whisk should get you through all your donut-baking needs.

Regular and mini nonstick donut pans: Standard donut pans yield 6 donuts, so for most of the recipes in this book you'll need to bake in batches or use two pans. A mini donut pan typically yields 12 mini donuts, and I recommend having one in your kitchen.

Donut and biscuit cutters: A standard-size donut cutter works for making regular shaped yeasted donuts (and donut holes), and a biscuit cutter makes quick work of forming donuts that can be filled. If you don't have a biscuit cutter, you can also use a round 5-inch cookie cutter.

Reusable pastry bags and tips: I recommend having an assortment of pastry bag sizes on hand, including 16- or 18-inch bags to fill donut pans and 12-inch bags to fill stuffed donuts with creams or jellies. You won't need a decorating tip to fill donut pans (just cut about 1 inch off the end of your bag and pipe that way), but for filling donuts, I do recommend having

⅞-inch "cream piping nozzle" to inject the filling from the pastry bag into the donut. You can easily find these online or at specialty baking stores.

Half-sheet pan: A standard rimmed baking sheet is also known as a half-sheet pan and measures about 18 by 13 inches. I recommend having two on hand if space allows, but one should be sufficient for the recipes in this book.

Digital kitchen scale: I have a standard 22-pound digital kitchen scale that I use for all baking. It's small, stores easily, and can usually be found for under $25 on Amazon or other online stores.

Mini donut maker: I used the Dash Mini Donut Maker to test recipes for this book, but any brand will work just as well. Be sure to read the manufacturer's instructions regarding general use and care, and always only fill the cavities to their specifications.

LOVE YOUR OVEN

Ovens are very personal, and getting to know your oven and how it works will help ensure the best possible results for your donuts. I recently replaced my oven because my old one was running "hot," meaning that my baked goods would dry out and get dark around the edges well before the stated bake time in the recipe had elapsed.

If you're noticing consistently overdone results when you bake (cookies burn on the bottom before the tops set; cakes, muffins, or donuts are dark and dry or crumbly), adjust your baking temperature to 25°F lower than what the recipe calls for and bake for a little bit longer. So, for example, if a recipe says to bake at 350°F for 15 minutes, but your oven runs hot, then bake at 325°F for 20 minutes instead. It's also a good idea to have your oven serviced if this is happening consistently, as it could mean there's an issue with the internal thermostat that needs adjusting.

Depending on where you live and whether your oven is conventional or convection, you may need to adjust the recipes in this book to make them work for you. If you live anywhere that is 3,000 feet or higher above sea level, that's a high-altitude area. Because air pressure is lower at higher altitudes, you will need to adjust ingredient quantities for baked goods to rise evenly. This means lowering the amount of chemical leaveners and increasing the volume of liquid in your batter.

For high-altitude baking, make the following adjustments to your baking recipes:

- Reduce baking powder in recipes by ⅛ teaspoon for every teaspoon used
- Reduce sugar by 1 tablespoon for every cup used
- For each cup of liquid used, add 1 to 2 tablespoons
- Increase your oven temperature by 25°F

A convection oven uses a fan and exhaust system to circulate hot air evenly throughout the oven, which a conventional or still oven does not. If you bake using a convection oven, you don't have to adjust the ingredient quantities to make any of the recipes in this book, but you will need to lower your oven temperature by 25°F.

ESSENTIAL TECHNIQUES

If you've never made a donut before, the mere thought of trying can be intimidating. And if we were talking about frying donuts, I might tend to agree. That's why I love baked donuts. If you've ever baked a muffin, a cupcake, or even a banana bread, you'll feel right at home making almost any recipe in this book.

I've designed this book to start out with simple baked donuts and work our way up to yeasted ones, because although they aren't as complex as fried donuts, they do require a little bit of extra work and different techniques to make them successful.

Proofing

Yeasted donuts, like anything else made with yeast, need time to proof (or rise) before baking. This is because the yeast is the active leavening agent, and it works more slowly than chemical leaveners like baking soda or baking powder. Proofing is a two-step process and requires time—so make sure you've got plenty of it before you start baking. Donuts can be proofed one of two ways: in a low-temperature oven or at room temperature. Doing it at room temperature takes longer, but it doesn't require turning on an oven. For the yeast donuts in this book, we'll be proofing twice: once as a dough and then again after the donuts are cut.

Rolling

Cake donuts don't require rolling, but yeast donuts do. That's because yeast donuts are made from dough rather than batter and can't be piped into donut pans. They need to be rolled like biscuit or cookie dough and cut out using donut or biscuit cutters. Yeast donuts grow in size by being proofed after they are cut. We'll typically roll the dough out to about ½ inch thick before cutting.

Cutting

Speaking of cutting, donut and biscuit cutters are your best friends when making yeast donuts. For regular yeast donuts, you would typically use a donut cutter to form the dough into rings (and to make donut holes from the leftovers!). Filled donuts are more of a bun or biscuit shape and are easily shaped by using a biscuit cutter. Mini cutters are also fun for making mini or bite-size donuts.

Filling

Yeast donuts are less sweet than their cake-based counterparts, because the dough has less butter and sugar in it, which means that when eaten plain, they tend to have a mild, almost tangy flavor. That's why you'll typically see yeast donuts covered in glaze or filled with jelly or cream or other flavorings. To fill a yeast donut with jelly or cream easily, I recommend using a "cream piping nozzle," a specialized long, thin tip that attaches to a regular pastry piping bag, which you can buy online or at specialty baking stores. This is a long, narrow nozzle that pushes through the side of the donut into the center of the donut to fill it. Alternatively, you can also use pastry bags fitted with regular round piping tips and fill the donut from the bottom or side, but you won't get as much filling in, because the round tip isn't as long as a piping nozzle.

Glazing

Glazing is where donuts really get their personality—and a lot of their flavor. In this book we'll explore different ways to glaze donuts, from dunking to drizzling. Dunking is typically used when you only want the top half of the donut covered. This works well for cake donuts that have lots of flavor in the actual donut itself. Drizzled or drenched donuts are typically yeast donuts that have glaze poured over them to coat the entire donut. The trick to attaining that thick, shiny glaze is to make sure your donuts are completely cooled before you start. If the donut has any residual heat in it, the glaze will melt right into the donut.

ESSENTIAL INGREDIENTS FOR A HEALTHY SWEET TOOTH

One of the best things about making donuts at home is that they don't need a lot of fancy ingredients. If you've got flour, sugar, baking powder, salt, and vanilla extract, you're halfway there! That being said, the quality of the ingredients you use will make a huge difference in the taste, texture, and overall success of your donuts.

Obviously, donuts are indulgent treats, and because we're making baked donuts, we are eliminating the oil and deep-frying element, which makes them a little bit healthier. But baked donuts require other less healthy ingredients, like a fair bit of flour and sugar. Because I want this book to appeal to as many specific diets as possible, I've looked for ways to include alternatives for flours, sugars, and other items to help keep these donuts on the (slightly) healthier side.

Below I've included lists of all my favorite easy-to-find-and-use vegan baking replacements. I'll use a variety of these in the recipes throughout this book.

Flours

All-purpose flour: The most common flour and typically the one most used in baking, all-purpose flour is milled from a mix of hard and soft wheat and works for all types of baked goods, like cakes, cookies, biscuits, pizza dough, muffins, and more. It's widely available at all grocery stores. If possible, try to choose an unbleached flour, as the bleaching process, which makes the flour whiter, also strips out some of the nutrients in the flour.

Whole-wheat flour: Wheat or whole-wheat flour is made from the entire wheat kernel, making it a healthier option than all-purpose. Whole-wheat flour is denser and heavier and has a slight nuttiness to it. Baking with whole-wheat flour won't yield the same airiness or sponge as all-purpose, but it's a good alternative if you want to reduce your white flour intake.

Spelt or light spelt flour: I like using light spelt flour as an alternative to (or in combination with) all-purpose flour. It is an ancient grain that is similar to wheat but with more protein. Regular spelt flour is heavy and dense, but light spelt is slightly refined to strip away the tough outer hull and is a great substitute for all-purpose flour in baking. If you want to achieve a cake-like texture in your donuts without using all-purpose flour, swap it out for light spelt.

Gluten-free all-purpose flour:
Gluten-free baking is incredibly easy now thanks to the availability of 1:1 all-purpose gluten-free flours. When I bake for my husband (who is gluten-free), I use a 1:1 flour like Bob's Red Mill. It mimics the texture and consistency of regular all-purpose flour and is a great substitute in any of the cake donuts in this book. You can find gluten-free all-purpose flour at most grocery stores and online.

Almond flour: Another gluten-free option, almond flour is made from very finely milled blanched almonds. Almond flour is quite moist and should always be stored in the refrigerator to keep it fresh. Almond flour doesn't always work as a 1:1 substitution flour, because it has no protein structure to hold it together. If you do decide to bake with only almond flour, you can start with a 1:1 substitution and then add more almond flour as needed to thicken the batter. Almond flour also requires more binders (aquafaba, banana, applesauce) to hold it together, so you'll need to adjust accordingly.

Leaveners

Baking soda: Baking soda is a white powder sold in boxes in grocery stores (most commonly in an iconic orange box) that, when mixed with an acidic ingredient like vinegar, lemon juice, or brown sugar, reacts to form carbon dioxide, which helps leaven the dough. Baking soda is a quick-acting leavener, meaning that in its dry state in the box, it's inert, but as soon as it mixes with an acid, it releases carbon dioxide that causes baked goods to rise.

Baking powder: Baking powder is a mix of baking soda and acids that, when added to wet ingredients, begins a chemical reaction to produce carbon dioxide that makes baked goods rise. Baking powder works in two ways in that it starts the leavening reaction when added to wet ingredients and again when heated. It doesn't work as fast as baking soda, though. Many recipes call for both baking soda and baking powder to be used together, because the amount of carbon dioxide that baking soda and an acidic ingredient in the recipe produce isn't enough to leaven the batter.

Yeast: Yeast is a biological leavening agent, because it's "alive" and feeds on sugar and starch to grow, which helps baked goods rise. Yeast comes in many forms, from active to quick-rise (or instant). It's available in jars or packets at all grocery stores and online. Typically, most baking recipes, like the ones in this book, will use active dry yeast, which requires time for proofing before baking.

Flavor Additions

Spices: Dried spices are a great way to add flavor to baked donuts, particularly ones made with cake batter. I like to keep a variety of baking spices on hand, like cinnamon, nutmeg, ginger, and cloves. Spice mixes are an inexpensive way to keep multiple spices on hand without taking up too much pantry space. Opt for spice mixes like gingerbread, pumpkin pie spice, or chai to get the warm flavors of fall baking.

Extracts: Good-quality extracts are a baker's best friend. Vanilla is the most common and is a must-have for your pantry. Always choose real or natural vanilla extract instead of artificial, which uses sugar alcohol and other chemicals to recreate the scent of vanilla without using any actual vanilla. Other extracts that are good to have on hand for baking are almond, lemon, orange, and peppermint. A little goes a long way with extracts, so be sure to measure them exactly.

Maple syrup: True maple syrup (not pancake syrup) is a great way to flavor donuts and also makes a great replacement for honey or refined sugars. I'm Canadian, so you can bet my pantry and my baked goods always have maple syrup in them! Buy a good-quality maple syrup and store it in the refrigerator for best results.

Molasses: Molasses is a thick, dark syrup that is created during the sugar-making process when sugarcane or sugar beets are boiled. Molasses contains a handful of vitamins, minerals, and antioxidants and adds a rich, nutty, and yeasty flavor to baked goods, and is paired most commonly with those with gingerbread flavors. What I really like about molasses is that it's not as sweet as sugar and can be used as a replacement for refined sugar while adding rich flavor.

Jams and jellies: Most yeast donuts would be nothing more than biscuits if it weren't for the jelly filling! I like to use seedless jams or canned pie fillings to fill and flavor donuts. They also work well in glazes, as in the Blueberry Glazed Donuts (page 70) or the Blackberry-Basil-Ricotta Donuts (page 78). Unopened, both jams and canned pie fillings are shelf stable and will last for a long time, making them a great addition to your baking pantry.

Chocolate: Chocolate can be used in a variety of ways to add flavor to baked donuts. I recommend having cocoa powder on hand for flavoring cake batter. For glazes, frostings, and even fillings (hello, chocolate ganache), keep dairy-free chocolate chips and chocolate chunks in your pantry. Always check labels first, but many semisweet chocolate chips and chunks are accidentally vegan and are widely available at most grocery stores. Dairy-free white chocolate chips (which you can easily find online) are great for making white chocolate glazes and frostings.

Nuts and nut butters: As long as nuts aren't an issue in your home, they are a great way to add texture and flavor to baked donuts. Nut butters, like peanut or almond, are great to add to cake donut batter, as part of a filling for filled yeast donuts, or as a frosting or drizzle on top of glazed donuts. Chopped nuts (peanuts, pecans, walnuts) sprinkled on top of a glazed donut taste as good as they look.

Coffee: Coffee and chocolate go hand in hand. Instant coffee powder and brewed espresso are great flavor boosters and help make chocolate cake donuts shine. The best thing about coffee is that it's in almost everyone's kitchen already. For a rich chocolate cake donut, add 1 teaspoon of instant coffee granules to the batter. Coffee also works well as part of a glaze (as in the Coffee-Caramel Nut Crunch Donuts, page 56).

Curds and custards: Vegan lemon or orange curds and vegan custards are actually quite easy to make. I've shared my homemade lemon curd recipe for the Lemon Meringue Donuts (page 80). Some custard powders, like Bird's, can be made vegan by swapping out regular milk for a plant-based alternative. It's a handy trick for making the Boston Cream Donuts (page 76).

Fruits: Fresh fruit (either picked ripe or flash frozen) is fantastic for making glazes. The Blueberry Glazed Donuts (page 70) are made with real blueberries in and on the donut, and fresh strawberries elevate the Strawberry Shortcake Donut Stacks (page 132) to absolute superstar status. Bananas in particular are a great match for donuts, because they add banana flavor and also act as a binder in place of eggs.

Citrus zest: The flavorful natural oils in lemon, orange, lime, and grapefruit peels are excellent ways to add a tart punch to donuts, like the Winter Cranberry-Orange Donuts (page 36) or the Coconut Key Lime Pie Donuts (page 60). I recommend using a really fine citrus zester (also called a rasp) when zesting citrus fruits to make sure you only get the colored peel and not the bitter, white pith underneath.

Binders

Flaxseed: Flax is incredibly healthy for you. It has healthy fats, antioxidants, and fiber and definitely boosts any dish. Ground flaxseed mixed with warm water forms a paste known as a "flax egg" and is a natural, easy substitute for eggs in baking. The typical ratio for a flax egg is 1 tablespoon of ground flaxseed mixed with 2 tablespoons of hot water and left to stand for 5 minutes. This is equal to 1 large egg.

Chia seeds: Like flax eggs, egg replacers made from chia seeds also help bind baked goods. Chia seeds are darker in color, so they will stand out a bit more in your donuts (unless you're making chocolate ones), but they also have huge health benefits. One large egg is equal to 1 tablespoon of chia seeds mixed with 3 tablespoons of water and left to stand for 15 minutes.

Bananas: Bananas are a great (and delicious) substitute for eggs. And if you're like me, you've always got some spotted, overripe ones hanging around on the kitchen counter. As a general rule, one mashed banana equals one large egg in baked goods. Pro tip: If you have more bananas than you need, peel the extras, cut them into large slices, and freeze them in a freezer-safe container or bag, then thaw them on the counter at room temperature a couple of hours before you start your bake.

Applesauce: Applesauce works triple duty when it comes to baking, because it can be used to bind and thicken a batter and as a great substitute for refined sugar. Because apples are naturally sweet, choose unsweetened applesauce for baking. Here's a helpful hint: Individual snack-size applesauce containers hold ¼ cup of applesauce, which is usually the perfect amount for replacing 1 large egg. If your recipe calls for more than 3 eggs, use a different egg replacer to replace the extra eggs, as too much applesauce can make your batter very runny.

Powdered egg replacers: Powdered egg replacers are commonly made from a mix of potato and tapioca starches and baking soda. When a small amount is mixed with water and left to thicken, it forms a binder that works like flax eggs do in holding baked goods together. It is also neutral in flavor, so it won't alter the desired taste of your donuts or other baked goods. Powdered egg replacers are readily available in supermarkets, but since each brand is slightly different, always refer to the package instructions before mixing.

Aquafaba: If you've been draining the liquid from canned chickpeas all these years, stop! That brine (called aquafaba or "bean water") has the same properties as an egg white and is a vegan baking game-changer. In its raw state (right from the can), it's a binding agent that replaces eggs at a ratio of 3 tablespoons of aquafaba for each egg. When whipped with sugar and cream of tartar, it's virtually indistinguishable from egg white meringue. Amazing, right?

Dairy Replacements and Fats

Plant-based milks: There are so many options available for swapping out dairy milk in vegan baking—and the best part is that they are all so readily available. As a general rule, stick to plain, unsweetened versions of whichever plant milk you use, so that you don't affect the flavor of your donut or add unnecessary sugar. I prefer to use unsweetened almond, soy, or oat milk in my baking. Avoid "thin" plant milks like rice milk, as they don't have much structure to them and won't hold a batter together.

Coconut milk: Canned coconut milk is a great substitute for traditional dairy and adds sweetness to baked donuts. I do recommend using full-fat coconut milk (and shaking the can really well before opening), because the natural fat in the coconut helps give stability to the batter.

Coconut cream: Coconut cream is the thick, solid, creamy part of coconut milk that you often find at the top of the can. It naturally separates from the watery part until shaken or stirred. You can now buy whole cans of just the coconut cream, which is excellent for making vegan whipped cream. Pro tip: Coconut cream needs to be cold to whip, so it's a good idea to always keep a can or two of coconut cream and milk in the refrigerator.

Soy cream: Soy cream is a vegan alternative to heavy cream. Belsoy makes one that is specifically for cooking and baking, and it's a great substitute if you don't like coconut cream. Silk makes an alternative creamer that is typically used in coffee, but it works well in baked goods, too.

Vegan butter: There are many brands of dairy-free or vegan butter and margarine available in almost every grocery store, and they work well as a 1:1 replacement for traditional butter. You can find vegan butter in tubs, blocks, and baking sticks, which are handy for easy measuring.

Vegan cream cheese: Vegan cheese has grown in popularity, making it readily available in most grocery stores. Vegan cream cheese typically falls into one of two categories: nut-based (cashew) or nut-free (coconut oil/soy-based). I prefer using nut-free cream cheeses for baking, because they don't impart any flavor, and their soy or coconut oil base has more of the necessary fat in it to help hold the donut together. Nut-based cream cheeses are typically cultured and/or aged and can have a tangy, almost earthy flavor to them, which can affect how your donuts taste.

Vegetable oil: Vegetable oil is a neutral oil that doesn't impart flavor to baked goods and is likely to already be in your pantry. It's a good replacement for vegan butter in cake batter donuts.

Coconut oil: Coconut oil has grown in popularity and is often used as a replacement for traditional vegetable or canola oil. It pairs well with chocolate and is good to have on hand for adding a smooth and shiny texture to chocolate glazes (think Lamington Donut Holes, page 130).

Avocados: Known as the "healthy fat," avocados can replace butter or oil in batters. If you're swapping out butter or oil for avocado, use a 1:1 ratio and adjust your baking temperature and time. A good rule of thumb is to bake at 25°F lower and for 5 to 10 minutes longer. Be aware that if you're using avocado in light-colored batters, like vanilla, your donuts will take on a greenish hue.

Sugars and Natural Sweeteners

Applesauce: Applesauce makes a great substitute for refined sugar when baking, without altering the flavor profile of the dish. Because apples are naturally sweet, I prefer to choose unsweetened applesauce for baking.

Granulated sugar: The most common and widely used in baking, granulated sugar is refined white sugar made from either sugarcane or sugar beets. It's widely available, extremely inexpensive, and neutral in flavor. Beet sugar is always vegan, but regular cane sugar can be processed using bone char, so it's a good idea to choose an organic one or do a little research into common grocery store brands to make sure the one you're using is vegan.

Coconut sugar: An alternative to refined white sugar, coconut sugar is also known as "raw sugar," because it's an unrefined sugar. It is slightly healthier than granulated sugar in that it's less refined and less sweet. It also contains minor amounts of nutrients. You can swap coconut sugar for granulated sugar at a 1:1 ratio.

Brown sugar: Despite what most people think, brown sugar isn't healthier than granulated. It's basically granulated sugar with molasses added to it. It has a rich, deep flavor that is almost nutty, and it works well in baked goods that have cinnamon and/or nuts in them. Brown sugar varies in color based on how much molasses is added. The darker the sugar, the sweeter it is.

Agave syrup: Agave is a plant-based sweetener often used to replace honey because of its golden sheen, stickiness, and light, neutral flavor. It can also be used to replace granulated sugar in baking. Agave is low on the glycemic index, making it a good option for diabetic or low-sugar baking. Because it's naturally sweeter than granulated sugar, you can use less of it when baking.

Dates: While I wouldn't recommend using dates in a batter, they are a great natural replacement for sugar in sauces. Dates have calcium, potassium, antioxidants, and vitamin A, making them a healthier option. I like to use Medjool dates to make caramel sauce.

Maple syrup: It's not just for pancakes! Maple syrup (the real stuff—not "pancake syrup") is a great alternative to refined sugar when baking. Not only does it add great flavor, but you'll need less of it to sweeten your donuts, making it a healthier option.

Monk fruit sweetener: Extracted from monk fruit, a South Asian fruit, monk fruit sweetener is extremely sweet, about 200 times sweeter than refined sugar, and 100 percent natural. It has become a sweetener of choice for low-sugar and low-calorie baking, as it contains zero calories. If you're baking with monk fruit sweetener, start with ⅓ cup of sweetener for every 1 cup of sugar and adjust if needed.

VEGAN DONUTS TROUBLESHOOTING

If you haven't baked donuts before, or you're just new to vegan baking in general, it can seem like an intimidating task. I'm here to help dispel that myth and coach you through how to make successful baked donuts. In this section I'll share some tips and tricks to help troubleshoot any issues you may have and give some pointers on how to ensure a successful bake. The good news is that baked donuts are actually quite easy, especially cake batter versions, so there's no need to be apprehensive.

   With the right tools (a mixing bowl, a spatula, and a donut pan) and good-quality ingredients, you can make delicious and healthy-ish donuts right in your own kitchen. You might even be inspired to open your own donut shop! Here are my top 5 troubleshooting tips:

1. **My donuts are dark and crumbly or hard:** Your oven is likely running hot, or there's a hot spot in your oven. Try baking your donuts at 25°F lower than the recipe calls for and for 5 to 10 minutes longer. Also, if your oven has a convection setting, make sure you didn't accidentally bake the donuts that way.

2. **My donuts crumbled when I removed them from the pan:** Always make sure to cool donuts completely before removing them from the donut pan. If they are too warm, they won't hold their shape and will crumble when removed. Also be sure to use a nonstick donut pan and/or lightly grease or spray the pan before adding the batter.

3. **My donut glaze is thin and runny:** You've likely added too much liquid to your glaze. Stir in more powdered sugar (1 tablespoon at a time) until the desired thickness is achieved.

4. **I'm making frosting and/or whipped cream for my donuts, but it won't whip/hold together:** Always start with cold coconut or soy cream when making whipped toppings or frostings. The best way to ensure you've got cold coconut cream at the ready is to stash a couple of cans at the back of your refrigerator, because who has time to wait for cream to chill? No one, that's who!

5. **I made yeast donuts, but they didn't rise:** Check the expiration date on your yeast. An opened container of yeast will only last for about 4 months before it expires and needs replacing. Unopened yeast can last up to a year. If you don't use yeast that often, consider buying a couple of single-use packets rather than an entire jar. Also make sure that you activated your yeast with warm (not hot) water. Hot water kills the yeast before it gets a chance to activate. The ideal temperature for activating yeast is between 110°F and 115°F.

VEGAN BAKING SECRETS

While there are inherent differences in the ingredients used for vegan desserts, apart from that, most of the techniques and tips for creating them are similar to their nonvegan counterparts. Here are a few quick tips that will serve you well as a baker, vegan or not!

Zest first, juice later. Adding both the zest and juice of citrus fruits to a donut is a great way to boost the flavor, but you should always zest your fruit first, then squeeze out the juice. The firmness of the full fruit makes it easier to shave off the zest.

Just chill! Proper cooling time is essential for delicious donuts. Always allow them to cool completely before stacking or frosting, as the residual heat can turn your buttercream into a butter pool or suck your glaze right off the top of your donut.

Temperature is key. Unless specifically stated otherwise (like for coconut cream whipped cream, which should be chilled), bringing ingredients like vegan butter and vegan cream cheese to room temperature before using them is important. If they're too cold, they won't mix properly, leaving you with grainy frostings or lumpy batter.

Conquer chocolate. Just like nonvegan chocolate, semisweet or dark dairy-free chocolate requires a bit of coddling when used in baking—particularly when it comes to heating, so take your time. Never melt chocolate over direct heat; instead, set up a double boiler (a heatproof glass bowl set on top of a pot of simmering water). Place the chocolate in the glass bowl, and let the residual heat and steam gently melt the chocolate. If using a microwave, heat the chocolate in a microwave-safe glass bowl in 30-second increments, stirring after each session, for a maximum of 1½ minutes. After that, remove the bowl from the microwave and stir to melt any leftover solids.

TIPS FOR SUCCESSFUL BAKING

We are almost ready to start baking! But before we do, I thought I'd share a few tips for ensuring your donuts come out deliciously perfect every time. If you're an experienced baker, you may already know these, but if you're a novice to vegan baking or to the world of baked donuts, these tips will help remove any anxiety or concerns you have about baking these delicious ringed treats.

1. **Read the ENTIRE recipe before starting:** There is nothing worse than getting halfway through a recipe and realizing that you're missing an ingredient or a specific tool—or that you needed to chill a component overnight. When I'm approaching a new recipe, I like to read through it twice: once with an eye for what ingredients are needed (so I can check my pantry and refrigerator for items I'll need to buy) and a second time to fully understand all the steps and processes involved—like chilling dough overnight!

2. **Set up your "mise en place":** Earlier in the book we talked about "mise en place" or "everything in place." Simply put, this means having all your ingredients, measuring and mixing tools, and baking pans ready to go BEFORE you start baking, so that you don't have to interrupt your baking multiple times to look for the cinnamon or line a baking sheet with parchment paper.

3. **Preheat your oven at the start:** Ovens take time to preheat, and nothing slows a bake down faster than sitting around waiting for yours to come to temperature. When I'm cooking, I'll use the preheat time to start cooking my food, as it helps shave a few minutes off my cook time. But that principle does not hold true for baking. Baking requires consistent temperature, and the fluctuation in temperature during preheating can cause your donuts to bake unevenly.

4. **Never open your oven:** For ovens (both conventional and convection) to remain at a constant temperature, they need to be left alone. As tempting as it is to peek at your treats midbake, you must resist! Opening the oven will cool it down, causing your donuts to deflate. If you must peek, switch on the light and look through the glass in the oven door.

ABOUT THE RECIPES

Okay, one more set of helpful hints and then it's time to get those spatulas working! I've broken down this book by different types of donuts, starting with the easiest (plain and sugared) and working up to more involved "donut-like" desserts such as éclairs, beignets, and fritters. So, if you're new to donut making, you can start off with some easy cake donuts until you get the hang of it, and then work your way up to yeast donuts or fancier treats.

I've used labels and tips throughout the book to help you get the best results and figure out which recipes fit your dietary needs or tickle your taste buds the most.

You'll find the following labels on the recipes in this book:

Gluten-free: Recipes that are designed to be made with gluten-free flour. (Note that many of the recipes in this book can be adapted for gluten-free baking, but the recipes with these labels are those where we've specifically chosen to share the naturally gluten-free version.) Always check ingredient packaging for gluten-free labeling to ensure that foods were processed in a completely gluten-free facility.

Low refined sugar or refined-sugar-free: Recipes that do not use white or brown granulated sugar or only call for small amounts in the topping or glaze will have one of these labels. These recipes rely on natural sweeteners like applesauce, monk fruit sweetener, raw coconut sugar, or maple syrup to add sweetness to the batter.

Many of the recipes in this book contain tips to highlight an ingredient, offer a variation on the recipe, or provide helpful information like where to find or how to shop for an ingredient. I've used the following tips in this book:

Ingredient tip: Highlights a particular ingredient, its uses or origins, and where to buy it or how to shop for it.

Variation tip: Suggests how to vary the flavor profile, adapt the recipe for allergy-friendly baking, or substitute alternatives for out-of-season ingredients.

Lighten up tip: Gives ideas on how to make the recipe lighter or lower in sugar, salt, or fat by substituting ingredients or adapting another technique.

**Chai Latte Donuts,
page 26**

CHAPTER 2

——

PLAIN AND SUGARED DONUTS

Chai Latte Donuts **26**

State Fair Mini Donuts **28**

Churro Donuts **30**

Gingerbread Donuts **32**

Chocolate Chip Banana Bread Donuts **34**

Winter Cranberry-Orange Donuts **36**

Chocolate-Coconut Donuts **38**

Salted Pecan Pie Donuts **40**

Mocha Sugar Donuts **42**

Spicy Hot Chocolate Donuts **44**

CHAI LATTE DONUTS

PREP TIME: 20 minutes • **COOK TIME:** 20 minutes
MAKES 12 DONUTS / 36 MINI DONUTS

Chai latte is the new ultimate sugared donut. Based on the flavors of Indian chai tea, these donuts use a mixture of aromatic spices such as cinnamon, ginger, cloves, cardamom, and allspice to give them a rich, exotic flavor before they are dipped in warm butter and coated in a cinnamon-sugar mix for that classic sugared donut texture.

FOR THE DONUTS

Vegan butter or nonstick cooking
  spray, for greasing the pans
2 cups (240 grams) all-purpose flour
½ cup (100 grams) granulated sugar
2 teaspoons chai spice mix
2 teaspoons baking powder

½ teaspoon baking soda
1⅓ cups unsweetened nondairy milk
¼ cup coconut oil, melted and slightly
  cooled
1 teaspoon vanilla extract

FOR THE TOPPING

4 tablespoons (½ stick) vegan butter
¼ cup (50 grams) granulated sugar

½ teaspoon ground cinnamon

1. **To make the donuts:** Preheat the oven to 350°F. Lightly grease with butter or spray with cooking spray 2 (6-cavity) donut pans or 3 (12-cavity) mini donut pans and set aside.

2. In a large mixing bowl, combine the flour, sugar, spice mix, baking powder, and baking soda. Pour in the milk, then add the coconut oil and vanilla. Mix with a rubber spatula until just combined, being careful not to overmix.

3. Spoon the batter into a pastry bag or a large resealable bag with a 1-inch hole cut in the corner. Pipe the batter into the prepared pans, filling each well half full.

4. Bake for 15 to 18 minutes (10 to 12 minutes for mini donuts, 7 to 8 minutes for donut makers), until a cake tester or toothpick inserted into the center comes out clean.

5. **To make the topping:** While the donuts are cooling, in a medium microwave-safe bowl, microwave the butter for 30 seconds, or until melted. In a separate medium bowl, mix the sugar and cinnamon. Gently brush each donut with melted butter, then roll in the cinnamon-sugar mix to coat.

INGREDIENT TIP: If you're having trouble finding a chai spice mix (not to be confused with a chai tea powder or concentrate!), you can substitute apple pie or pumpkin pie spice mix.

PER FULL-SIZE DONUT: Calories: 207; Total fat: 9g; Saturated fat: 5g; Cholesterol: 0g; Sodium: 68mg; Carbohydrates: 30g; Fiber: 1g; Sugar: 13g; Protein: 3g

STATE FAIR MINI DONUTS

PREP TIME: 15 minutes • **COOK TIME:** 15 minutes
MAKES 36 MINI DONUTS

Mini donuts covered in icing sugar (which is what powdered sugar is called in Canada) are probably the most iconic state fair or carnival food ever. Every August when I was growing up, I would visit the Canadian National Exhibition in my hometown of Toronto, and my first stop was always the mini donut truck. This recipe turns that nostalgic treat into a delicious homemade snack perfect for sharing.

Vegan butter or nonstick cooking
  spray, for greasing the pans
1¼ cups unsweetened nondairy milk
¾ cup (150 grams) granulated sugar
4 tablespoons (½ stick) vegan butter,
  melted

1½ teaspoons baking powder
1 teaspoon baking soda
1 teaspoon vanilla extract
2 cups (240 grams) all-purpose flour
½ cup (57 grams) powdered sugar

1. Preheat the oven to 350°F. Lightly grease with butter or spray with cooking spray 3 (12-cavity) mini donut pans and set aside.

2. In a large mixing bowl, whisk together the milk, granulated sugar, melted butter, baking powder, baking soda, and vanilla.

3. Switch to a rubber spatula and gently fold in the flour, mixing until just combined. The batter may be a bit lumpy—that's okay!

4. Spoon the batter into the prepared pans, or transfer it to a large resealable bag or pastry bag and pipe it into the pans, filling each well half full.

5. Bake for 10 to 14 minutes, until fluffy. Cool in the pan for 5 minutes, then transfer to a wire rack to cool almost completely.

6. Once the donuts have cooled, place the powdered sugar into a shallow, wide dish and add the donuts in batches, tossing to coat.

VARIATION TIP: Switch up these fairground classics by swapping out the powdered sugar for a blend of ½ cup (100 grams) of granulated sugar and ½ teaspoon of ground cinnamon.

PER MINI DONUT: Calories: 61; Total fat: 1g; Saturated fat: 0g; Cholesterol: 0g; Sodium: 55mg; Carbohydrates: 11g; Fiber: 0g; Sugar: 6g; Protein: 1g

CHURRO DONUTS

PREP TIME: 15 minutes • **COOK TIME:** 15 minutes
LOW REFINED SUGAR
MAKES 12 DONUTS / 36 MINI DONUTS

Imagine taking all the delicious cinnamon and fried-dough flavor of a churro and turning it into a healthy-ish baked donut instead. That's what I've done here. As well as avoiding all the oil from deep-frying, these cake donuts get their sweetness from applesauce instead of refined sugar, which in my book means you get to eat more of them.

FOR THE DONUTS

¼ cup hot water
2 tablespoons ground flaxseed
¾ cup unsweetened nondairy milk
1 tablespoon freshly squeezed lemon juice or apple cider vinegar
Vegan butter or nonstick cooking spray, for greasing the pans
¼ cup plus 2 tablespoons unsweetened applesauce

2 tablespoons coconut oil, melted
1 teaspoon vanilla extract
2 cups (240 grams) light spelt or all-purpose flour
1½ teaspoons baking powder
1 teaspoon ground cinnamon
¼ teaspoon baking soda
¼ teaspoon ground nutmeg

FOR THE CINNAMON-SUGAR TOPPING

3 tablespoons vegan butter
½ cup (100 grams) granulated sugar

2 teaspoons ground cinnamon
¼ teaspoon ground nutmeg

1. **To make the donuts:** In a small bowl, combine the hot water and flaxseed and let stand 5 minutes to thicken. In a glass measuring cup, combine the milk and lemon juice and let stand 5 minutes.

2. While the flaxseed mixture and the milk mixture are resting, preheat the oven to 350°F. Lightly grease with butter or spray with cooking spray 2 (6-cavity) donut pans or 3 (12-cavity) mini donut pans and set aside.

3. Add the flaxseed mixture, applesauce, coconut oil, and vanilla to the milk mixture and whisk to combine.

4. In a large bowl, combine the flour, baking powder, cinnamon, baking soda, and nutmeg. Pour in the wet ingredients and stir until just combined.

5. Spoon the batter into the prepared pans, or transfer it to a piping bag or a resealable bag with a 1-inch hole cut in the corner and pipe it into the pans. Fill each well three-quarters full.

6. Bake for 10 to 12 minutes (8 to 10 minutes for mini donuts, 7 to 8 minutes for donut makers), or until the donuts are firm to the touch and a cake tester inserted into the center comes out clean. Cool in the pan for 5 minutes, then transfer to a wire rack until cool enough to hold but not cold.

7. **To make the cinnamon-sugar topping:** While the donuts are cooling, in a small microwave-safe bowl, melt the butter in the microwave for 15 to 20 seconds. In a wide, shallow bowl, combine the sugar, cinnamon, and nutmeg. Brush the donuts with melted butter and roll in the cinnamon-sugar mix to coat.

PER FULL-SIZE DONUT: Calories: 155; Total fat: 6g; Saturated fat: 3g; Cholesterol: 0g; Sodium: 82mg; Carbohydrates: 23g; Fiber: 1g; Sugar: 5g; Protein: 3g

GINGERBREAD DONUTS

PREP TIME: 10 minutes • **COOK TIME:** 15 minutes
MAKES 12 DONUTS / 36 MINI DONUTS

In my family, gingerbread is synonymous with Christmas, and this recipe has become a holiday favorite of ours. Full of classic winter baking flavors like nutmeg, clove, and ginger, these donuts are absolutely irresistible when watching holiday movies or gathering with friends. Try swapping out the cinnamon-sugar coating for a sugar glaze and cinnamon-sugar sprinkle, as in the Cinnamon and Apple Cider Glazed Donuts (page 48).

FOR THE DONUTS

2 tablespoons hot water

1 tablespoon ground flaxseed

Vegan butter or nonstick cooking spray, for greasing the pans

1¼ cups (150 grams) light spelt or all-purpose flour

½ teaspoon baking powder

1 teaspoon ground cinnamon

¼ teaspoon baking soda

⅛ teaspoon ground nutmeg

⅛ teaspoon ground cloves

⅛ teaspoon ground ginger

½ cup unsweetened nondairy milk

¼ cup (55 grams) packed brown sugar

¼ cup molasses

3 tablespoons unsweetened nondairy Greek-style yogurt, such as Daiya

2 tablespoons vegan butter, melted

FOR THE CINNAMON-SUGAR TOPPING

⅓ cup granulated sugar

½ teaspoon ground cinnamon

½ teaspoon ground ginger

¼ teaspoon ground nutmeg

4 tablespoons (½ stick) vegan butter, melted

1. **To make the donuts:** In a small bowl, combine the hot water and flaxseed and let stand for 5 minutes.

2. While the flaxseed mixture is resting, preheat the oven to 350°F. Lightly grease with butter or spray with cooking spray 2 (6-cavity) donut pans or 3 (12-cavity) mini donut pans and set aside.

3. In a large bowl, combine the flour, baking powder, cinnamon, baking soda, nutmeg, cloves, and ginger.

4. In a separate large bowl, whisk together the flaxseed mixture, milk, brown sugar, molasses, yogurt, and melted butter. (It's okay if there are tiny bits of yogurt in the batter.) Fold the flour mixture into the wet mixture, stirring until just combined.

5. Spoon the batter into the prepared pans, filling each well completely.

6. Bake for 13 to 15 minutes (8 to 10 minutes for mini donuts, 6 to 7 minutes for donut makers), or until the donuts spring back when lightly touched and/ or a cake tester inserted into the center comes out clean. Cool in the pan for 5 minutes, then transfer to a wire rack to cool for another few minutes.

7. **To make the cinnamon-sugar topping:** While the donuts are cooling, in a wide, shallow bowl, combine the sugar, cinnamon, ginger, and nutmeg. Brush the donuts with the melted butter and roll them in the sugar mixture.

INGREDIENT TIP: Gingerbread spices, in particular nutmeg, cloves, and ginger, are quite potent, and a little really goes a long way. If you don't want to take up extra space in your pantry, consider using a premade gingerbread spice mix instead.

PER FULL-SIZE DONUT: Calories: 170; Total fat: 6g; Saturated fat: 1g; Cholesterol: 0g; Sodium: 55mg; Carbohydrates: 27g; Fiber: 1g; Sugar: 15g; Protein: 2g

CHOCOLATE CHIP BANANA BREAD DONUTS

PREP TIME: 10 minutes • **COOK TIME:** 25 minutes
LOW REFINED SUGAR
MAKES 8 DONUTS

There's really nothing better than the smell of freshly baked banana bread wafting through your home, and it's matched by the natural sweetness banana lends to baked treats. I've turned my classic chocolate chip banana bread into delicious donuts that are the perfect size to snack on any time. A note for this recipe: I don't recommend adapting this recipe for mini donuts or a donut maker. It's a lumpy, sticky dough and is hard to manage in smaller equipment.

Vegan butter or nonstick cooking
  spray, for greasing the pans
1½ cups (180 grams) all-purpose flour
½ cup rolled oats
¼ cup (53 grams) lightly packed
  brown sugar
1 teaspoon baking soda
1 teaspoon baking powder
½ teaspoon salt

3 large ripe bananas
⅓ cup unsweetened nondairy milk
⅓ cup vegetable oil
2 tablespoons ground flaxseed
2 tablespoons maple syrup
1 tablespoon vanilla extract
1 cup dairy-free mini chocolate chips,
  divided (I prefer Enjoy Life brand)

1. Preheat the oven to 350°F. Lightly grease with butter or spray with cooking spray 2 (6-cavity) donut pans and set aside. Make sure to only grease 8 of the cavities.

2. In a large bowl, combine the flour, oats, brown sugar, baking soda, baking powder, and salt and mix well.

3. In a medium bowl, mash the bananas until almost no chunks remain. Add the milk, vegetable oil, flaxseed, maple syrup, and vanilla. Stir to combine.

4. Slowly pour the wet ingredients into the dry mixture and stir until just combined. Stir in ½ cup of mini chocolate chips.

5. Pour the cake batter into the donut pans, filling 8 of the cavities, and sprinkle the remaining ½ cup of mini chocolate chips evenly on top.

6. Bake for 20 to 25 minutes, until a cake tester inserted into the center comes out clean. Cool in the pan for 10 minutes, then transfer to a wire rack to continue cooling.

PER DONUT: Calories: 420; Total fat: 19g; Saturated fat: 6g; Cholesterol: 0g; Sodium: 353mg; Carbohydrates: 57g; Fiber: 5g; Sugar: 24g; Protein: 6g

WINTER CRANBERRY-ORANGE DONUTS

PREP TIME: 15 minutes • **COOK TIME:** 15 minutes
MAKES 12 DONUTS / 36 MINI DONUTS

This recipe started out as a muffin—a really soft and cake-like muffin that was just begging to be turned into a donut. I wanted it to fulfill its destiny, so I developed it to be perfect for these smaller baked treats. The addition of vanilla nondairy yogurt adds richness and flavor, but if you're not a fan of vegan yogurt, or you want to cut down on the fat content, swap it out for an equal amount of unsweetened applesauce.

Vegan butter or nonstick cooking
  spray, for greasing the pans
1 cup cranberries (fresh, or frozen
  and thawed)
2 tablespoons granulated sugar,
  plus ⅓ cup
2 cups (240 grams) light spelt flour
1 tablespoon baking powder

½ teaspoon baking soda
½ teaspoon ground ginger
Zest of 1 large orange
¾ cup freshly squeezed orange juice
  (from 2 oranges)
½ cup vanilla-flavored nondairy yogurt
2 tablespoons coconut oil, melted

1. Preheat the oven to 350°F. Lightly grease with butter or spray with cooking spray 2 (6-cavity) donut pans or 3 (12-cavity) mini donut pans and set aside.

2. In a food processor, combine the cranberries and 2 tablespoons of sugar and pulse until coarsely chopped. Set aside.

3. In a large bowl, combine the flour, remaining ⅓ cup of sugar, baking powder, baking soda, ginger, and orange zest. Add the orange juice, yogurt, coconut oil, and cranberry mixture. Stir until just combined.

4. Spoon the batter into the prepared pans.

5. Bake for 13 to 15 minutes (8 to 10 minutes for mini donuts, 5 to 7 minutes for donut makers), until the donuts are slightly golden and a cake tester inserted into the center comes out clean. Cool in the pan for 5 minutes, then transfer to a wire rack to cool completely.

VARIATION TIP: Give this classic holiday pairing an even fancier look by brushing the cooled donuts with melted vegan butter and rolling them in a mix of granulated sugar **AND CANDIED ORANGE PEEL.**

PER FULL-SIZE DONUT: Calories: 142; Total fat: 3g; Saturated fat: 2g; Cholesterol: 0g; Sodium: 148mg; Carbohydrates: 28g; Fiber: 3g; Sugar: 10g; Protein: 3g

CHOCOLATE-COCONUT DONUTS

PREP TIME: 20 minutes • **COOK TIME:** 15 minutes
MAKES 10 DONUTS / 30 MINI DONUTS

Chocolate cake donuts are my favorite, because they remind me of chocolate cake—only I don't have to share them! I was born on National Chocolate Cake Day, so it makes perfect sense that when I'm craving donuts, I reach for these. This is actually a phenomenal base for any chocolate donut, whether sugared or glazed, so definitely bookmark this page!

Vegan butter or nonstick cooking spray, for greasing the pans
2 cups (240 grams) all-purpose flour
½ cup (100 grams) granulated sugar
¼ cup (21 grams) dark cocoa powder
1 teaspoon baking powder
¼ teaspoon salt

¾ cup unsweetened nondairy milk
3 tablespoons coconut oil, melted
1 teaspoon vanilla extract
½ cup (85 grams) dairy-free semisweet chocolate chips
4 tablespoons (½ stick) vegan butter, melted
1 cup (85 grams) shredded coconut

1. Preheat the oven to 350°F. Lightly grease with butter or spray with cooking spray 2 (6-cavity) donut pans or 3 (12-cavity) mini donut pans and set aside.

2. In a large bowl, whisk together the flour, sugar, cocoa powder, baking powder, and salt. Pour in the milk, coconut oil, and vanilla and stir until just combined. Gently fold in the chocolate chips.

3. Spoon the batter into the prepared pans, filling each well three-quarters full.

4. Bake for 12 to 15 minutes (8 to 10 minutes for mini donuts, 5 to 7 minutes for donut makers), or until the donuts bounce back when lightly touched. Cool in the pan for 5 minutes.

5. Once the donuts have cooled, dip the donut tops only into the melted butter and then into the shredded coconut.

VARIATION TIP: For extra coconut flavor, swap out the nondairy milk for the same amount of full-fat canned coconut milk.

PER FULL-SIZE DONUT: Calories: 296; Total fat: 15g; Saturated fat: 9g; Cholesterol: 0g; Sodium: 108mg; Carbohydrates: 37g; Fiber: 3g; Sugar: 14g; Protein: 4g

SALTED PECAN PIE DONUTS

PREP TIME: 30 minutes • **COOK TIME:** 30 minutes
MAKES 12 DONUTS / 36 MINI DONUTS

I don't think you can get a more indulgent donut than this one. It's part pecan pie, part brownie, and part donut, all in one delicious package. I've lowered the amount of sugar from my original recipe, though, so it isn't over-the-top sweet. I do recommend making the candied pecans in advance, because they take a while to cool. They can be stored in an airtight container for a week at room temperature.

FOR THE CANDIED PECANS
3 tablespoons brown sugar
1 tablespoon water
1 teaspoon ground cinnamon
¼ teaspoon sea salt
¼ teaspoon vanilla extract
1 cup pecan halves

FOR THE DONUTS
½ cup hot water
¼ cup ground flaxseed
Vegan butter or nonstick cooking spray, for greasing the pans
8 tablespoons (1 stick) vegan butter, melted
½ cup (100 grams) coconut sugar
½ cup (106 grams) lightly packed brown sugar
1 tablespoon vanilla extract
1 cup (120 grams) all-purpose flour
1 cup (84 grams) dark cocoa powder
1 teaspoon instant coffee granules
1 teaspoon baking powder
¼ teaspoon kosher salt
1 cup (170 grams) dairy-free semisweet chocolate chips

1. **To make the candied pecans:** Line a sheet pan with parchment paper and set aside.

2. In a medium saucepan combine the brown sugar, water, cinnamon, salt, and vanilla, and cook over medium heat, stirring frequently, for about 1 minute, or until the brown sugar is liquid and bubbling.

3. Stir in the pecans until completely coated and continue cooking for about 2 minutes, or until they look shiny and smell nutty.

4. Remove from the heat, spread out on the prepared baking sheet, and allow to cool completely. Once the pecans have cooled, chop them into small pieces that can be mixed into a batter.

5. **To make the donuts:** In a small bowl, combine the hot water and flaxseed and let stand for 5 minutes to thicken.

6. While the flaxseed mixture is resting, preheat the oven to 350°F. Lightly grease with butter or spray with cooking spray 2 (6-cavity) donut pans or 3 (12-cavity) mini donut pans and set aside.

7. In a large bowl, whisk to combine the flaxseed mixture, melted butter, coconut sugar, brown sugar, and vanilla. Add the flour, cocoa powder, coffee, baking powder, and salt and stir until the mixture is just combined and you can't see any traces of flour. Gently fold in the chocolate chips and candied pecan pieces.

8. Use a spoon to fill the donut pans three-quarters full of batter.

9. Bake for 20 to 22 minutes (15 to 17 minutes for mini donuts). Don't worry if the tops look a little underdone. Like any good brownie, they set up perfectly once cooled. Cool completely before removing from the pan.

PER FULL-SIZE DONUT: Calories: 354; Total fat: 21g; Saturated fat: 6g; Cholesterol: 0g; Sodium: 92mg; Carbohydrates: 42g; Fiber: 5g; Sugar: 25g; Protein: 4g

MOCHA SUGAR DONUTS

PREP TIME: 15 minutes • **COOK TIME:** 15 minutes
MAKES 6 DONUTS / 18 MINI DONUTS

Coffee and donuts go hand in hand, so it makes perfect sense to create a donut that is made with coffee. These fluffy mocha sugar donuts have just the right amount of sweetness and coffee flavor and are perfect any time of day. I like them coated in sugar, but they are also delicious with a light vanilla (or espresso) glaze.

2 tablespoons hot water
1 tablespoon ground flaxseed
Vegan butter or nonstick cooking spray, for greasing the pans
1½ cups (180 grams) all-purpose or light spelt flour
½ cup (42 grams) dark cocoa powder
⅓ cup (70 grams) lightly packed brown sugar
1 tablespoon instant espresso powder
½ teaspoon baking powder

½ teaspoon baking soda
½ teaspoon kosher salt
⅓ cup unsweetened nondairy milk
⅓ cup unsweetened nondairy Greek-style yogurt
⅓ cup vegetable oil
1½ teaspoons vanilla extract
½ cup dairy-free espresso chips, such as Bakers Choice or other kosher brands
⅓ cup granulated sugar, for coating

1. In a small bowl, combine the hot water and flaxseed and let stand for 5 minutes.

2. While the flaxseed mixture is resting, preheat the oven to 350°F. Lightly grease with butter or spray with cooking spray 1 (6-cavity) donut pan or 2 (12-cavity) mini donut pans and set aside.

3. In a large bowl, whisk together the flour, cocoa powder, brown sugar, espresso powder, baking powder, baking soda, and salt. Set aside.

4. In another large bowl, whisk to combine the flaxseed mixture, milk, yogurt, vegetable oil, and vanilla. Gently fold the dry ingredients into the wet ingredients, being careful not to overmix the batter. Stir in the espresso chips.

5. Transfer the batter to a pastry bag or a resealable bag with a 1-inch hole cut in the corner and pipe it into the prepared pan, filling each well two-thirds full.

6. Bake for 12 to 15 minutes (8 to 10 minutes for mini donuts, 5 to 7 minutes for donut makers), until a cake tester or toothpick inserted into the center comes out clean. Cool in the pan on a wire rack for 8 to 10 minutes, or until cool enough to handle.

7. Place the granulated sugar in a shallow dish and gently roll each donut in the sugar while still warm.

INGREDIENT TIP: Look for kosher espresso chips or mocha-flavored chips in kosher grocery stores or online. Kosher dietary laws prohibit the mixing of meat and milk products in a meal, so many kosher baking ingredients are made "pareve" or without dairy, so that they can be served with either meal.

PER FULL-SIZE DONUT: Calories: 330; Total fat: 14g; Saturated fat: 2g; Cholesterol: 0g; Sodium: 250mg; Carbohydrates: 49g; Fiber: 3g; Sugar: 18g; Protein: 6g

SPICY HOT CHOCOLATE DONUTS

PREP TIME: 25 minutes • **COOK TIME:** 15 minutes
MAKES 12 DONUTS / 36 MINI DONUTS

Chocolate and cayenne are a wonderful combination. These donuts are super chocolaty and have just enough heat to tickle your tastebuds and stand out from ordinary chocolate donuts. I love making these on cold winter nights. Donuts on their own are fun, but these are even more so, because they come with their own dipping sauce.

FOR THE DONUTS

Vegan butter or nonstick cooking spray, for greasing the pans
2 cups (240 grams) all-purpose flour
½ cup (100 grams) granulated sugar
¼ cup (21 grams) dark cocoa powder
1 teaspoon instant coffee granules
1 teaspoon baking powder
¼ teaspoon ground cinnamon

¼ teaspoon ground cayenne pepper
¼ teaspoon salt
1 cup unsweetened nondairy milk
3 tablespoons coconut oil, melted
1 teaspoon vanilla extract
½ cup (85 grams) dairy-free semisweet chocolate chips

FOR THE CHOCOLATE DIP

½ cup (85 grams) dairy-free semisweet chocolate chips
½ cup coconut cream, at room temperature

¼ teaspoon ground cinnamon
⅛ to ¼ teaspoon ground cayenne pepper

1. **To make the donuts:** Preheat the oven to 350°F. Lightly grease 2 (6-cavity) donut pans or 3 (12-cavity) mini donut pans and set aside.

2. In a large bowl, whisk together the flour, sugar, cocoa powder, coffee, baking powder, cinnamon, cayenne, and salt. Pour in the milk, coconut oil, and vanilla and stir until just combined. Gently fold in the chocolate chips.

3. Spoon the batter into the prepared pans, filling each well three-quarters full.

4. Bake for 12 to 15 minutes (8 to 10 minutes for mini donuts, 5 to 7 minutes for donut makers), or until the donuts bounce back when lightly touched. Cool in the pan for 5 minutes, then transfer to a wire rack to cool completely.

5. **To make the chocolate dip:** Place the chocolate chips in a heatproof bowl. Pour the coconut cream into a small saucepan and heat over medium heat until steaming but not boiling. Remove from the heat and pour over the chocolate chips. Let stand for 1 to 2 minutes, then gently stir the chocolate, letting the heat from the cream melt it. Once the chocolate has melted, add the cinnamon and cayenne. Serve with the donuts for dipping.

VARIATION TIP: If you're not a huge fan of cayenne pepper, swap it out for an equal amount of extra cinnamon and add a pinch of ginger or nutmeg instead.

PER FULL-SIZE DONUT: Calories: 265; Total fat: 13g; Saturated fat: 9g; Cholesterol: 0g; Sodium: 91mg; Carbohydrates: 34g; Fiber: 3g; Sugar: 14g; Protein: 4g

London Fog Donuts, page 62; Chocolate Peppermint-Bark-Glazed Donuts, page 68

CHAPTER 3

GLAZED AND FROSTED DONUTS

Cinnamon and Apple Cider Glazed Donuts 48

Vanilla-Glazed Coffee Cake Donuts 50

Donut Shop Glazed Donuts 52

Double Chocolate Frosted Donuts 54

Coffee-Caramel Nut Crunch Donuts 56

Cherry-Glazed D'oh! Nuts 58

Coconut Key Lime Pie Donuts 60

London Fog Donuts 62

Lemon-Poppyseed Glazed Donuts 64

Maple-Coconut-"Bacon"-Glazed Donuts 66

Chocolate Peppermint-Bark-Glazed Donuts 68

Blueberry Glazed Donuts 70

Zucchini Donuts with
Cream Cheese Frosting 72

CINNAMON AND APPLE CIDER GLAZED DONUTS

PREP TIME: 10 minutes • **COOK TIME:** 10 minutes
GLUTEN-FREE OPTION
MAKES 6 DONUTS / 18 MINI DONUTS

Apple cider always reminds me of autumn, and these donuts are the perfect treat after a fun fall day apple picking or jumping in piles of leaves. The cinnamon-sugar sprinkle on top of the glaze adds great texture and flavor, but if you're looking for an option with less refined sugar, you can swap out the granulated sugar for coconut sugar or skip the sprinkle altogether.

FOR THE DONUTS

Vegan butter or nonstick cooking spray, for greasing the pan(s)
1 cup (120 grams) all-purpose or gluten-free all-purpose flour
1½ teaspoons baking powder
½ teaspoon baking soda
½ teaspoon ground cinnamon
½ teaspoon kosher salt
⅛ teaspoon ground nutmeg

⅛ teaspoon ground cloves
⅛ teaspoon ground ginger
⅓ cup maple syrup
⅓ cup apple cider, strained to remove some of the liquid
¼ cup unsweetened applesauce
1 tablespoon vegetable oil
1 teaspoon vanilla extract

FOR THE GLAZE

½ cup powdered sugar

1 tablespoon apple cider

FOR THE CINNAMON-SUGAR SPRINKLE

¼ cup granulated sugar
2 teaspoons ground cinnamon

⅛ teaspoon ground nutmeg

1. **To make the donuts:** Preheat the oven to 350°F. Lightly grease with butter or spray with cooking spray 1 (6-cavity) donut pan or 2 (12-cavity) mini donut pans and set aside.

2. In a large bowl, combine the flour, baking powder, baking soda, cinnamon, salt, nutmeg, cloves, and ginger. Add the maple syrup, apple cider, apple-sauce, vegetable oil, and vanilla and stir until just combined, ensuring no streaks of flour remain.

3. Spoon the batter into a pastry bag or a large resealable bag with a 1-inch hole cut out of the corner and pipe it into the prepared pan, filling each well about three-quarters full. Alternatively, use a tablespoon to spoon the batter into the pan.

4. Bake for 8 to 10 minutes (5 to 7 minutes for mini donuts or donut makers), until the donuts spring back when lightly touched. Cool in the pan for 5 minutes, then transfer to a wire rack to cool completely.

5. **To make the glaze:** While the donuts are cooling, in a small bowl, whisk together the powdered sugar and apple cider until a thick but pourable glaze forms.

6. **To make the cinnamon-sugar sprinkle:** In another small bowl, mix the granulated sugar, cinnamon, and nutmeg together. Dip the top of each donut in the glaze (or drizzle the glaze on the donuts with a spoon for a less sweet version), then sprinkle with the cinnamon-sugar mix.

PER FULL-SIZE DONUT: Calories: 220; Total fat: 3g; Saturated fat: 0g; Cholesterol: 0g; Sodium: 296mg; Carbohydrates: 46g; Fiber: 1g; Sugar: 28g; Protein: 2g

VANILLA-GLAZED COFFEE CAKE DONUTS

PREP TIME: 15 minutes • **COOK TIME:** 15 minutes
MAKES 6 DONUTS / 18 MINI DONUTS

This donut combines the classic flavors and textures of a coffee cake in a handheld version that you don't have to share! Coffee cake traditionally uses full-fat sour cream to give it a rich, dense texture. I've lightened this up a bit by swapping out the sour cream for nondairy yogurt instead.

FOR THE STREUSEL TOPPING
¼ cup granulated sugar
3½ tablespoons all-purpose flour
2 tablespoons vegan butter, cold, diced
¼ teaspoon ground cinnamon

FOR THE DONUTS
2 tablespoons hot water
1 tablespoon ground flaxseed
Vegan butter or nonstick cooking spray, for greasing the pans
1 cup (120 grams) all-purpose flour
½ cup (110 grams) packed brown sugar
1 teaspoon baking powder
1 teaspoon ground cinnamon
½ teaspoon salt
½ cup unsweetened nondairy yogurt
2 tablespoons vegetable oil

FOR THE VANILLA GLAZE
½ cup powdered sugar
½ tablespoon unsweetened plain or vanilla nondairy milk
½ teaspoon vanilla extract

1. **To make the streusel topping:** In a small bowl, combine the sugar, flour, butter, and cinnamon, mashing it together using a fork until it resembles a coarse crumb. Set aside.

2. **To make the donuts:** In a small bowl, combine the hot water and flaxseed and let stand for 5 minutes to thicken.

3. While the flaxseed mixture is resting, preheat the oven to 350°F. Lightly grease with butter or spray with cooking spray 1 (6-cavity) donut pan or 2 (12-cavity) mini donut pans and set aside.

4. In a large bowl, gently whisk together the flour, brown sugar, baking powder, cinnamon, and salt. Add the flaxseed mixture, yogurt, and vegetable oil and stir until the mixture is just combined and no flour streaks remain. Transfer the batter to a pastry bag or a resealable bag with a 1-inch hole cut in the corner and pipe it into the prepared pan, filling each well two-thirds full. Alternatively, spoon the batter into the pan. Divide the streusel topping evenly across the top of all the donuts.

5. Bake for 10 to 11 minutes (7 to 9 minutes for mini donuts), until a cake tester inserted into the center comes out clean. Cool in the pan for 10 minutes, then transfer to a wire rack with a sheet pan lined with parchment or wax paper underneath.

6. **To make the vanilla glaze:** While the donuts are cooling, in a small bowl, combine the powdered sugar, milk, and vanilla and whisk until a thick but pourable glaze forms. Drizzle the glaze over each donut before serving.

PER FULL-SIZE DONUT: Calories: 330; Total fat: 9g; Saturated fat: 2g; Cholesterol: 0g; Sodium: 270mg; Carbohydrates: 58g; Fiber: 1g; Sugar: 35g; Protein: 4g

DONUT SHOP GLAZED DONUTS

PREP TIME: 10 minutes • **COOK TIME:** 15 minutes
GLUTEN-FREE
MAKES 12 DONUTS / 36 MINI DONUTS

My husband had a passionate love affair with Krispy Kreme in his youth. Let's be honest, most of us did (and some of us still do!). That's why I created this copycat of their iconic original glazed donut. Since my husband is now gluten-free, I made this one with gluten-free flour for him to enjoy, but if gluten isn't a concern for you, swap in regular self-rising flour instead.

FOR THE DONUTS

Vegan butter or nonstick cooking spray, for greasing the pans
2½ cups (300 grams) gluten-free self-rising flour

1 cup unsweetened nondairy milk
½ cup maple syrup or agave syrup
¼ cup vegetable oil

FOR THE GLAZE

2 cups powdered sugar
1 teaspoon vanilla extract

1 to 3 tablespoons unsweetened nondairy milk

1. **To make the donuts:** Preheat the oven to 350°F. Lightly grease with butter or spray with cooking spray 2 (6-cavity) donut pans or 3 (12-cavity) mini donut pans and set aside.

2. In a large bowl, combine the flour, milk, maple syrup, and vegetable oil and stir to create a thick batter.

3. Spoon the batter into the prepared pans, filling each well about three-quarters full. Alternatively, pipe the batter into the pans with a pastry bag or a resealable bag with a 2-inch hole cut in the corner.

4. Bake for 12 to 15 minutes (8 to 10 minutes for mini donuts, 5 to 7 minutes for donut makers), until a cake tester inserted into the center comes out clean. Cool in the pan for 5 minutes, then transfer to a wire rack to cool completely.

5. **To make the glaze:** While the donuts are cooling, in a small bowl, combine the powdered sugar, vanilla, and 1 tablespoon of milk. Stir, gradually adding more milk, until a thick but pourable glaze forms.

6. Dip each cooled donut in the glaze and let set.

INGREDIENT TIP: Self-rising flour is flour that already has leavening agents in it, typically baking powder, and some salt. If you can't find self-rising flour, you can make your own by adding 1½ teaspoons of baking powder and ¼ teaspoon of salt to every cup of all-purpose flour.

PER FULL-SIZE DONUT: Calories: 239; Total fat: 5g; Saturated fat: 0g; Cholesterol: 0g; Sodium: 323mg; Carbohydrates: 46g; Fiber: 1g; Sugar: 25g; Protein: 3g

DOUBLE CHOCOLATE FROSTED DONUTS

PREP TIME: 20 minutes, plus 2 hours to chill the frosting • **COOK TIME:** 15 minutes
GLUTEN-FREE, REFINED-SUGAR-FREE
MAKES 12 DONUTS / 36 MINI DONUTS

Is there anything more indulgent than a chocolate donut covered in thick, rich chocolate frosting and topped with sprinkles? Aside from being gluten-free, this donut is also made without refined sugar, making it a healthier option. This recipe works well with regular self-rising flour, too, if gluten isn't an issue.

FOR THE CHOCOLATE GANACHE FROSTING

¾ cup coconut cream, cold

1½ cups (255 grams) dairy-free semisweet chocolate chips

FOR THE DONUTS

Vegan butter or nonstick cooking spray, for greasing the pans

2 cups (240 grams) gluten-free self-rising flour

½ cup (42 grams) dark cocoa powder

1 cup unsweetened nondairy milk

½ cup maple syrup

¼ cup vegetable oil

Sprinkles (optional), for topping

1. **To make the chocolate ganache frosting:** Place the coconut cream in a large bowl and set it aside.

2. In a microwave-safe bowl or glass measuring cup, microwave the chocolate chips in 30-second increments until melted, stirring after each turn to let the residual heat help melt the chocolate. Do not microwave more than three times (90 seconds total).

3. Add the melted chocolate to the coconut cream and whisk to combine. Cover with plastic wrap and refrigerate for a minimum of 2 hours (up to overnight) to thicken.

4. Remove the bowl from the refrigerator and use a hand mixer to whip the chocolate cream into a light and fluffy frosting.

5. **To make the donuts:** Preheat the oven to 350°F. Lightly grease with butter or spray with cooking spray 2 (6-cavity) donut pans or 3 (12-cavity) mini donut pans and set aside.

6. In a large bowl, whisk together the flour and cocoa powder. Add the milk, maple syrup, and vegetable oil and stir to create a thick batter.

7. Spoon the batter into the prepared pans, filling each well about three-quarters full. Alternatively, pipe the batter into the pans with a pastry bag or a resealable bag with a 2-inch hole cut in the corner.

8. Bake for 12 to 15 minutes (8 to 10 minutes for mini donuts, 5 to 7 minutes for donut makers), until a cake tester inserted into the center comes out clean. Cool in the pan for 5 minutes, then transfer to a wire rack to cool completely. Once the donuts have cooled, frost them and top them with the sprinkles (if using).

VARIATION TIP: Easily turn these donuts into chocolate-frosted vanilla donuts by skipping the cocoa powder and using 2½ cups of gluten-free self-rising flour and a splash of vanilla extract.

PER FULL-SIZE DONUT: Calories: 335; Total fat: 19g; Saturated fat: 10g; Cholesterol: 0g; Sodium: 263mg; Carbohydrates: 39g; Fiber: 4g; Sugar: 16g; Protein: 5g

COFFEE-CARAMEL NUT CRUNCH DONUTS

PREP TIME: 25 minutes, plus 30 minutes to cool the coffee toffee crunch
COOK TIME: 40 minutes
MAKES 12 DONUTS / 36 MINI DONUTS

Coffee and chocolate are a great combination because of the way each enhances the flavor of the other—any baker knows that the secret to a really good chocolate cake (or chocolate cake donuts) is to add coffee. This recipe does that and more by adding a coffee-flavored toffee nut crunch and a chocolate-coffee glaze. The toffee crunch takes a bit of time, so consider making it up to a day ahead—just store it in an airtight container at room temperature until needed.

FOR THE COFFEE TOFFEE CRUNCH

½ cup (106 grams) lightly packed brown sugar
⅓ cup (40 grams) all-purpose flour
1 teaspoon dark cocoa powder
1 teaspoon instant coffee granules
¼ teaspoon salt
4 tablespoons (½ stick) vegan butter, cold
½ cup (57 grams) finely chopped almonds or pecans

FOR THE DONUTS

2 tablespoons hot water
1 tablespoon ground flaxseed
Vegan butter or nonstick cooking spray, for greasing the pans
1½ cups (180 grams) all-purpose flour
½ cup (42 grams) dark cocoa powder
⅓ cup (67 grams) coconut sugar
2 teaspoons instant coffee granules
½ teaspoon baking powder
½ teaspoon baking soda
½ teaspoon salt
⅓ cup unsweetened nondairy yogurt
⅓ cup unsweetened nondairy milk
⅓ cup vegetable oil
1 teaspoon vanilla extract

FOR THE CHOCOLATE GLAZE

¼ cup (42 grams) dark chocolate chips
1 teaspoon instant coffee granules
1 teaspoon unsweetened nondairy milk

1. **To make the coffee toffee crunch:** Preheat the oven to 350°F and line a sheet pan with parchment paper.

2. In a small bowl, combine the brown sugar, flour, cocoa powder, coffee, and salt. Add the butter and use a pastry cutter to cut the butter into the flour mix until it is the size of small peas. Transfer to the prepared baking sheet and spread in an even layer.

3. Bake for 25 minutes, stopping halfway to stir the mixture. Remove from the oven and mix in the chopped nuts. Let the mix cool to room temperature, then transfer to a resealable bag and gently roll a rolling pin over the bag to break up any large chunks. Transfer to a shallow plate and set aside.

4. **To make the donuts:** In a small bowl, combine the hot water and flaxseed and let stand for 5 minutes.

5. While the flaxseed mixture is resting, preheat the oven to 350°F. Lightly grease with butter or spray with cooking spray 2 (6-cavity) donut pans or 3 (12-cavity) mini donut pans and set aside.

6. In a large bowl, combine the flour, cocoa powder, coconut sugar, coffee, baking powder, baking soda, and salt. Add the flaxseed mixture, yogurt, milk, vegetable oil, and vanilla and stir until just combined. Pipe or spoon the batter into the prepared pans, filling each well about two-thirds full.

7. Bake for 11 to 12 minutes (7 to 8 minutes for mini donuts, 5 to 6 minutes for donut makers), until a cake tester inserted into the center comes out clean. Cool in the pan for 5 minutes, then transfer to a wire rack to cool.

8. **To make the chocolate glaze:** Place the chocolate chips in a microwave-safe bowl and heat for 30 seconds, stirring to let the residual heat melt the chocolate. Add the instant coffee and milk and whisk until smooth and pourable.

9. Dip the top of each donut into the chocolate glaze, then immediately into the toffee crunch.

PER FULL-SIZE DONUT: Calories: 288; Total fat: 16g; Saturated fat: 3g; Cholesterol: 0g; Sodium: 225mg; Carbohydrates: 35g; Fiber: 3g; Sugar: 16g; Protein: 4g

CHERRY-GLAZED D'OH! NUTS

PREP TIME: 15 minutes • **COOK TIME:** 15 minutes
GLUTEN-FREE OPTION
MAKES 6 DONUTS / 18 MINI DONUTS

With their soft, cakey vanilla batter and neon pink tart cherry glaze, these sprinkle-covered d'oh-nuts look just like the ones Homer Simpson loves. I recommend using gel food coloring to achieve that hot, bright pink color. Both Wilton and Chefmaster make gel food coloring that is vegan-friendly and easy to find in stores and online.

FOR THE DONUTS

2 tablespoons hot water
1 tablespoon ground flaxseed
Vegan butter or nonstick cooking spray, for greasing the pan(s)
⅓ cup (66 grams) granulated sugar
4 tablespoons (½ stick) vegan butter, at room temperature

1 cup (120 grams) light spelt flour or gluten-free all-purpose flour
⅓ cup unsweetened nondairy milk
1 teaspoon vanilla extract
1 teaspoon baking powder
¼ teaspoon salt

FOR THE CHERRY GLAZE

1½ cups (170 grams) powdered sugar
3 tablespoons maraschino cherry juice
4 maraschino cherries, very finely chopped
½ teaspoon unsweetened nondairy milk (preferably almond milk; see the ingredient tip)

2 or 3 drops bright pink gel food coloring
Rainbow sprinkles (optional), for decoration

1. **To make the donuts:** In a small bowl, combine the hot water and flaxseed. Stir and let stand for 5 minutes to thicken.

2. While the flaxseed mixture is resting, preheat the oven to 350°F. Lightly grease with butter or spray with cooking spray 1 (6-cavity) donut pan or 2 (12-cavity) mini donut pans and set aside.

3. In a large mixing bowl, cream together the sugar and butter for about 5 minutes, or until light and fluffy. Add the flaxseed mixture, flour, milk, vanilla, baking powder, and salt and beat for about 2 minutes, or until fully combined.

4. Transfer the batter to a pastry bag or a resealable bag with a 1-inch hole cut in the corner and pipe it into the prepared pan, filling each well about two-thirds full. Alternatively, spoon the batter into the pan.

5. Bake for 10 to 13 minutes (7 to 8 minutes for mini donuts, 5 to 7 minutes for donut makers), until a cake tester inserted into the center comes out clean. Cool in the pan for 5 minutes, then transfer to a wire rack on top of a lined baking sheet to continue cooling.

6. **To make the cherry glaze:** While the donuts are cooling, in a medium bowl, combine the powdered sugar, cherry juice, chopped cherries, milk, and food coloring. Whisk until a thick but pourable glaze forms. Dip the top of each donut into the glaze and place back on the wire rack. Garnish with the sprinkles (if using).

INGREDIENT TIP: Many recipes that call for cherries or cherry juice also add almond flavoring (almond extract or almond milk), because cherry and almond are extremely complementary flavors. I recommend using almond milk in the glaze to boost the cherry flavor, but if nuts are a concern, you can replace it with an equal amount of cherry juice or use soy milk instead.

PER FULL-SIZE DONUT: Calories: 301; Total fat: 8g; Saturated fat: 1g; Cholesterol: 0g; Sodium: 168mg; Carbohydrates: 54g; Fiber: 1g; Sugar: 37g; Protein: 3g

COCONUT KEY LIME PIE DONUTS

PREP TIME: 10 minutes • **COOK TIME:** 15 minutes
MAKES 6 DONUTS / 18 MINI DONUTS

My dad is a Floridian and a true Key lime pie aficionado. He will turn down almost any other dessert if Key lime pie is an option. He also loves donuts, so I challenged myself to create the ultimate Key lime pie donut for when he comes to visit. For extra flair, fancy this donut up by toasting the shredded coconut before dipping the donuts in it.

FOR THE DONUTS
2 tablespoons hot water
1 tablespoon ground flaxseed
Vegan butter or nonstick cooking spray, for greasing the pan(s)
1 cup (120 grams) all-purpose flour
½ cup (100 grams) coconut sugar
1 teaspoon baking powder
Zest and juice of 2 Key limes
½ teaspoon salt
½ cup unsweetened nondairy coconut yogurt
2 tablespoons vegetable oil
½ teaspoon coconut extract (optional)

FOR THE COCONUT GLAZE
½ cup powdered sugar
3½ teaspoons coconut milk
½ teaspoon vanilla extract
1 cup unsweetened shredded coconut
Zest of 2 Key limes

1. **To make the donuts:** In a small bowl, combine the hot water and flaxseed and let stand for 5 minutes to thicken.

2. While the flaxseed mixture is resting, preheat the oven to 350°F. Lightly grease with butter or spray with cooking spray 1 (6-cavity) donut pan or 2 (12-cavity) mini donut pans and set aside.

3. In a large bowl, gently whisk together the flour, coconut sugar, baking powder, lime zest, and salt. Add the flaxseed mixture, lime juice, yogurt, vegetable oil, and coconut extract (if using) and stir until the ingredients are just combined and no flour streaks remain.

4. Transfer the batter to a pastry bag or a resealable bag with a 1-inch hole cut in the corner and pipe it into the prepared pan, filling each well two-thirds full. Alternatively, spoon the batter into the pan.

5. Bake for 12 to 14 minutes (7 to 9 minutes for mini donuts), until a cake tester inserted into the center comes out clean. Cool in the pan for 10 minutes, then transfer to a wire rack set in a sheet pan lined with parchment or wax paper.

6. **To make the coconut glaze:** While the donuts are cooling, in a small bowl, combine the powdered sugar, milk, and vanilla and whisk until a thick but pourable glaze forms. Place the shredded coconut on a plate and toss it with the lime zest.

7. Dip the top of each donut in the glaze and then in the shredded coconut.

INGREDIENT TIP: Key limes are the smaller, tarter cousins of the traditional limes we know and love. They have an intense sweet-and-sour flavor that pairs well with the richness of coconut. Key limes are available in most grocery stores, but they have a short growing season (June to September).

PER FULL-SIZE DONUT: Calories: 301; Total fat: 11g; Saturated fat: 5g; Cholesterol: 0g; Sodium: 267mg; Carbohydrates: 48g; Fiber: 2g; Sugar: 26g; Protein: 4g

LONDON FOG DONUTS

PREP TIME: 20 minutes • **COOK TIME:** 10 minutes
MAKES 10 DONUTS

London Fog is a classic Canadian drink, originating in Vancouver. It's essentially a latte, but instead of being made with espresso, it's made with Earl Grey tea (a floral tea that has notes of bergamot and lavender), vanilla syrup, and steamed milk. It also makes a fabulous, light, and delicate donut perfect for afternoon tea.

2 tablespoons hot water

1 tablespoon ground flaxseed

1 cup unsweetened plain or vanilla nondairy milk

3 Earl Grey tea bags

Vegan butter or nonstick cooking spray, for greasing the pans

1½ cups (180 grams) all-purpose flour

1½ teaspoons baking powder

½ teaspoon baking soda

¼ teaspoon salt

½ cup unsweetened applesauce

3 tablespoons vegan butter, melted

1 teaspoon vanilla extract

1 cup powdered sugar

1 or 2 drops lavender gel food coloring (optional)

Purple sanding sugar, for decoration (optional)

1. In a small bowl, combine the hot water and flaxseed and let stand for 5 minutes to thicken.

2. In a small saucepan, heat the milk over medium heat until steaming but not boiling. Remove from the heat and add the tea bags, then cover and steep for 5 minutes.

3. While the flaxseed mixture is resting and the milk is steeping, preheat the oven to 350°F. Lightly grease with butter or spray with cooking spray 2 (6-cavity) donut pans and set aside.

4. In a large bowl, combine the flour, baking powder, baking soda, and salt. Add ½ cup of the steeped milk (discarding the tea bags), the flaxseed mixture, applesauce, melted butter, and vanilla and gently stir to form the dough. If the mix is too dry, add 1 to 2 more tablespoons of the steeped milk, making sure to reserve 2 tablespoons for the glaze.

5. Transfer the batter to a pastry bag or a resealable bag with a 1-inch hole cut in the corner and pipe it into the prepared pans, filling each well about three-quarters full. Alternatively, spoon the batter into the pans.

6. Bake for 8 to 10 minutes, until a cake tester inserted into the center comes out clean. Cool in the pan for 5 minutes, then transfer to a wire rack to continue cooling.

7. While the donuts are cooling, in a small bowl, combine the powdered sugar with the remaining 2 tablespoons of the steeped milk and the food coloring (if using). Stir or whisk until a thick but pourable glaze forms.

8. Dip the top of each donut into the glaze and then sprinkle with the sanding sugar (if using).

PER DONUT: Calories: 152; Total fat: 4g; Saturated fat: 1g; Cholesterol: 0g; Sodium: 184mg; Carbohydrates: 27g; Fiber: 1g; Sugar: 11g; Protein: 2g

LEMON-POPPYSEED GLAZED DONUTS

PREP TIME: 15 minutes • **COOK TIME:** 15 minutes
MAKES 12 DONUTS / 36 MINI DONUTS

I love the classic combination of lemon and poppyseed. Bright, tangy lemon plays so well with these savory little seeds, and this donut is one of the best ways to highlight this flavor pairing. I've incorporated lemon juice into both the donut and the glaze to maximize its punchy, tart flavor.

FOR THE DONUTS

Vegan butter or nonstick cooking spray, for greasing the pans
2 cups (240 grams) all-purpose flour
½ cup (100 grams) granulated sugar
2 tablespoons poppyseeds
1 tablespoon grated lemon zest
2 teaspoons baking powder
½ teaspoon baking soda
¼ teaspoon salt
1⅓ cups unsweetened nondairy milk
3 tablespoons coconut oil, melted
2 tablespoons freshly squeezed lemon juice

FOR THE GLAZE

1 cup (113 grams) powdered sugar, plus extra if needed
1 tablespoon freshly squeezed lemon juice
½ teaspoon vanilla extract
1 to 2 tablespoons unsweetened nondairy milk
2 teaspoons poppyseeds (optional), for garnish

1. **To make the donuts:** Preheat the oven to 400°F. Lightly grease with butter or spray with cooking spray 2 (6-cavity) donut pans or 3 (12-cavity) mini donut pans and set aside.

2. In a large bowl, whisk together the flour, sugar, poppyseeds, lemon zest, baking powder, baking soda, and salt. Add the milk, coconut oil, and lemon juice and mix until the ingredients are just combined and no flour streaks are left. Transfer the batter to a pastry bag or a resealable bag with a 1-inch hole cut in the corner and pipe it into the prepared pans, filling each well two-thirds full.

3. Bake for 10 to 12 minutes (7 to 9 minutes for mini donuts, 5 to 7 minutes for donut makers), until a cake tester inserted into the center comes out clean. Cool in the pan for 5 minutes, then transfer to a wire rack to continue cooling.

4. **To make the glaze:** While the donuts are cooling, in a small bowl, combine the powdered sugar, lemon juice, vanilla, and 1 tablespoon of milk until an opaque, pourable glaze forms. If the mixture is too thick, add the remaining 1 tablespoon of milk. If it's too runny, add more powdered sugar, 1 tablespoon at a time.

5. Dip the top of each donut into the glaze, then return to the wire rack. Sprinkle with the poppyseeds (if using).

PER FULL-SIZE DONUT: Calories: 188; Total fat: 4g; Saturated fat: 3g; Cholesterol: 0g; Sodium: 176mg; Carbohydrates: 34g; Fiber: 1g; Sugar: 17g; Protein: 3g

MAPLE-COCONUT-"BACON"-GLAZED DONUTS

PREP TIME: 20 minutes • **COOK TIME:** 30 minutes
MAKES 10 DONUTS / 30 MINI DONUTS

Bacon donuts started becoming popular just as I was becoming vegan. Not wanting to miss out on any new food trend, I figured out how to capture that smoky, sweet flavor and chewy texture of bacon in a plant-based way, using coconut. It's the perfect topping for these maple-glazed donuts.

FOR THE COCONUT BACON

3 cups large unsweetened coconut flakes or chips

2½ tablespoons reduced-sodium soy sauce

1½ tablespoons maple syrup

1 tablespoon liquid smoke

1 tablespoon coconut oil, melted

FOR THE DONUTS

Vegan butter or nonstick cooking spray, for greasing the pans

½ cup unsweetened nondairy milk

½ teaspoon freshly squeezed lemon juice

1¼ cups (150 grams) all-purpose flour

2 teaspoons baking powder

½ teaspoon baking soda

½ teaspoon ground cinnamon

½ teaspoon salt

⅛ teaspoon ground nutmeg

½ cup (100 grams) coconut sugar

½ cup unsweetened plain nondairy yogurt

¼ cup coconut oil, melted

1 teaspoon vanilla extract

FOR THE GLAZE

1 cup (113 grams) powdered sugar

¼ cup maple syrup

1. **To make the coconut bacon:** Preheat the oven to 325°F. Line a large sheet pan with parchment paper and set aside.

2. In a large bowl, combine the coconut flakes, soy sauce, maple syrup, liquid smoke, and coconut oil and toss until well coated. Spread out evenly on the prepared baking sheet. Bake on the middle rack for 12 to 15 minutes, flipping

once halfway through. Coconut bacon goes from "done" to "burnt" quickly, so keep a close eye on it as it bakes. Remove from the oven and set aside to cool completely.

3. **To make the donuts:** Preheat the oven to 350°F. Lightly grease with butter or spray with cooking spray 2 (6-cavity) donut pans or 3 (12-cavity) mini donut pans and set aside.

4. In a glass measuring cup, combine the milk and lemon juice and let stand for 5 minutes.

5. While the milk is standing, in a large bowl, whisk together the flour, baking powder, baking soda, cinnamon, salt, and nutmeg.

6. In a smaller bowl, whisk together the milk mixture, coconut sugar, yogurt, coconut oil, and vanilla. Pour the wet mixture into the flour mixture and stir until the ingredients are just combined and no flour streaks are lef. Transfer the batter to a pastry bag or a resealable bag with a 1-inch hole cut in the corner and pipe it into the prepared pans, or spoon it into the pans, filling each well two-thirds full.

7. Bake for 12 to 15 minutes (8 to 10 minutes for mini donuts, 5 to 7 minutes for donut makers), until a cake tester inserted into the center comes out clean. Cool in the pan for 5 to 10 minutes, then transfer to a wire rack to cool.

8. **To make the glaze:** While the donuts are cooling, in a small bowl, whisk together the powdered sugar and maple syrup to form a thick but pourable glaze. Place the coconut bacon on a wide, shallow plate.

9. Dip the top of each donut into the glaze and then immediately into the coconut bacon flakes. Return to the wire rack to let the glaze set for 5 minutes.

INGREDIENT TIP: Coconut flakes (or chips) are large, flaked pieces of dried coconut and are used instead of shreds. You can find coconut flakes online or at most specialty stores like Whole Foods or Trader Joe's.

PER FULL-SIZE DONUT: Calories: 328; Total fat: 15g; Saturated fat: 13g; Cholesterol: 0g; Sodium: 397mg; Carbohydrates: 46g; Fiber: 3g; Sugar: 28g; Protein: 4g

CHOCOLATE PEPPERMINT-BARK-GLAZED DONUTS

PREP TIME: 10 minutes • **COOK TIME:** 15 minutes
MAKES 12 DONUTS / 36 MINI DONUTS

These rich, dark, chocolate-glazed donuts are my holiday go-to dessert. Sprinkling actual crushed candy canes on top of them adds a sparkly, holiday shine and a perfectly minty taste. Make these as mini donuts for your next holiday gathering, and I guarantee they'll become an instant favorite.

FOR THE DONUTS

Vegan butter or nonstick cooking spray, for greasing the pans
2 cups (240 grams) all-purpose flour
½ cup (100 grams) granulated sugar
¼ cup (21 grams) dark cocoa powder

1 teaspoon baking powder
¼ teaspoon salt
1 cup unsweetened nondairy milk
3 tablespoons coconut oil, melted
1 teaspoon vanilla extract

FOR THE GLAZE

1 cup (113 grams) powdered sugar
3 tablespoons dark cocoa powder
½ teaspoon vanilla extract
2 drops peppermint extract

3 to 4 tablespoons unsweetened nondairy milk
6 candy canes, crushed

1. **To make the donuts:** Preheat the oven to 350°F. Lightly grease with butter or spray with cooking spray 2 (6-cavity) donut pans or 3 (12-cavity) mini donut pans and set aside.

2. In a large bowl, whisk together the flour, sugar, cocoa powder, baking powder, and salt. Pour in the milk, coconut oil, and vanilla and stir until just combined.

3. Spoon the batter into the prepared pans, filling each well three-quarters full.

4. Bake for 12 to 15 minutes (8 to 10 minutes for mini donuts, 5 to 7 minutes for donut makers), until the donuts bounce back when lightly touched. Cool in the pan for 5 minutes, then transfer to a wire rack to continue cooling.

5. **To make the glaze:** While the donuts are cooling, in a small bowl, whisk together the powdered sugar, cocoa powder, vanilla, peppermint extract, and milk. Dip the tops of each donut into the glaze, then sprinkle with the crushed candy canes.

PER FULL-SIZE DONUT: Calories: 194; Total fat: 4g; Saturated fat: 3g; Cholesterol: 0g; Sodium: 88mg; Carbohydrates: 38g; Fiber: 2g; Sugar: 19g; Protein: 3g

BLUEBERRY GLAZED DONUTS

PREP TIME: 20 minutes • **COOK TIME:** 15 minutes
REFINED-SUGAR-FREE OPTION
MAKES 12 DONUTS / 36 MINI DONUTS

If you're a blueberry lover like me, you'll definitely want to indulge in these purple-hued donuts, which pack a one-two blueberry punch in the flavor department. Fresh blueberries are mixed into the batter of these baked cake donuts, and then they're topped with a delicious wild blueberry jam glaze.

FOR THE DONUTS

Vegan butter or nonstick cooking spray, for greasing the pans
2 cups (240 grams) light spelt flour
½ cup (100 grams) granulated sugar
2 teaspoons baking powder
1 teaspoon baking soda

1 teaspoon grated lemon zest
¼ teaspoon salt
1⅓ cups unsweetened nondairy milk
¼ cup vegetable oil
1 teaspoon vanilla extract
½ cup fresh blueberries

FOR THE GLAZE

2 cups (227 grams) powdered sugar
3 tablespoons unsweetened nondairy milk

2 tablespoons wild blueberry jam
1 teaspoon vanilla extract
⅛ teaspoon salt

1. **To make the donuts:** Preheat the oven to 400°F. Lightly grease with butter or spray with cooking spray 2 (6-cavity) donut pans or 3 (12-cavity) mini donut pans and set aside.

2. In a large bowl, combine the flour, sugar, baking powder, baking soda, lemon zest, and salt. Add the milk, vegetable oil, and vanilla and stir until the ingredients are just combined and no flour streaks are left. Gently fold in the blueberries.

3. Spoon the batter into the prepared pans, filling each well about three-quarters full.

4. Bake for 10 to 12 minutes (7 to 9 minutes for mini donuts), until a cake tester inserted into the center comes out clean. Cool in the pan for 5 minutes, then transfer to a wire rack to continue cooling.

5. **To make the glaze:** While the donuts are cooling, in a medium saucepan, combine the powdered sugar, milk, blueberry jam, vanilla, and salt over medium heat. Cook, whisking continuously, until combined.

6. Dip the tops of each donut into the glaze and return to the wire rack to set.

LIGHTEN UP TIP: Swap out the granulated sugar for an equal amount of unsweetened applesauce to reduce the sugar content of these donuts. Because you're swapping out a dry ingredient for a wet one, you'll also need to reduce the amount of nondairy milk to 1 cup. To make refined-sugar-free, omit the glaze.

PER FULL-SIZE DONUT: Calories: 238; Total fat: 5g; Saturated fat: 0g; Cholesterol: 0g; Sodium: 256mg; Carbohydrates: 45g; Fiber: 1g; Sugar: 28g; Protein: 3g

ZUCCHINI DONUTS WITH CREAM CHEESE FROSTING

PREP TIME: 20 minutes • **COOK TIME:** 10 minutes

LOW REFINED SUGAR

MAKES 6 DONUTS

I'm a mom of small kids who don't always love to eat vegetables—especially green ones. So sometimes I have to get creative about how I get them to eat their veggies. They are both big fans of zucchini muffins (especially chocolate ones) and zucchini bread, so I thought I'd try out a zucchini donut, too. I'm glad I did—because they love them almost as much as I do.

FOR THE DONUTS

2 tablespoons hot water

1 tablespoon ground flaxseed

Vegan butter or nonstick cooking spray, for greasing the pan

1 cup (120 grams) light spelt flour

⅓ cup (67 grams) coconut sugar

1 teaspoon baking powder

¼ teaspoon baking soda

¼ teaspoon kosher salt

¼ cup unsweetened nondairy Greek-style yogurt

¼ cup unsweetened nondairy milk

3 tablespoons coconut oil, melted

½ cup shredded zucchini (squeezed to remove excess water)

FOR THE CREAM CHEESE FROSTING

½ cup plain vegan cream cheese, at room temperature

3 tablespoons powdered sugar

2 tablespoons unsweetened plain nondairy milk

½ teaspoon vanilla extract

1 cup chopped pecans

1. **To make the donuts:** In a small bowl, combine the hot water and flaxseed and let stand 5 minutes to thicken.

2. While the flaxseed mixture is resting, preheat the oven to 350°F. Lightly grease with butter or spray with cooking spray 1 (6-cavity) donut pan and set aside.

3. In a medium bowl, whisk together the flour, coconut sugar, baking powder, baking soda, and salt. Add the yogurt, milk, and coconut oil and mix until the ingredients are just combined and no flour streaks are left in the batter. Gently fold in the shredded zucchini. Spoon the batter into the prepared pan, filling each well three-quarters full.

4. Bake for 10 minutes, or until a cake tester inserted into the center comes out clean. Cool in the pan for 10 minutes, then transfer to a wire rack to cool completely.

5. **To make the cream cheese frosting:** In a medium bowl, combine the cream cheese, powdered sugar, milk, and vanilla. Use a hand mixer on medium speed to cream the ingredients together.

6. Spread the frosting evenly on the top of each donut and sprinkle half of each donut with the chopped pecans.

PER DONUT: Calories: 404; Total fat: 26g; Saturated fat: 8g; Cholesterol: 0g; Sodium: 267mg; Carbohydrates: 38g; Fiber: 3g; Sugar: 18g; Protein: 6g

**Lemon Meringue
Donuts, page 80**

CHAPTER 4

FILLED DONUTS

Boston Cream Donuts **76**

Blackberry-Basil-Ricotta Donuts **78**

Lemon Meringue Donuts **80**

Stuffed S'mores Donuts **83**

Raspberry-Mango Donuts **86**

Strawberry Jelly Donuts **88**

Caramel Apple Pie Donuts **90**

Peach Streusel Donuts **93**

Cookies and Cream Donuts **96**

Coconut Custard Donuts **98**

BOSTON CREAM DONUTS

PREP TIME: 35 minutes, plus 1 hour 15 minutes for the dough to rise
COOK TIME: 25 minutes
MAKES 16 DONUTS

Boston cream donuts are the handheld version of the famed Boston cream pie, which originated in—yes, you guessed it—Boston, Massachusetts, in 1856. Typically filled with a vanilla custard and glazed with chocolate, these puffy yeast donuts have been an American classic ever since they were first made.

FOR THE CUSTARD FILLING
1 cup cashew milk
1 cup full-fat coconut milk
½ cup maple syrup

¼ cup cornstarch
1 tablespoon vanilla extract
⅛ teaspoon ground turmeric

FOR THE DONUTS
1¼ cups unsweetened nondairy milk
¼ cup (50 grams) coconut sugar
1 (¼-ounce) packet active dry yeast
½ cup unsweetened applesauce,
  at room temperature

¼ cup coconut oil, melted
1 teaspoon vanilla extract
1 teaspoon grated lemon zest
¼ teaspoon ground nutmeg
4½ cups (540 grams) all-purpose flour

FOR THE CHOCOLATE GLAZE
1 cup (113 grams) powdered sugar
3 tablespoons dark cocoa powder
½ teaspoon vanilla extract

4 tablespoons unsweetened
  nondairy milk

1. **To make the custard filling:** In a medium saucepan, combine the cashew milk, coconut milk, maple syrup, cornstarch, vanilla, and turmeric over medium heat. Simmer for 6 to 9 minutes, whisking constantly, until thickened. Remove from the heat and let cool completely. Once the filling has cooled, transfer it to a pastry bag fitted with a cream piping nozzle and refrigerate until needed.

2. **To make the donuts:** In a small microwave-safe bowl, microwave the milk for 1 minute, or until steaming but not scalding or boiling. Transfer to a large bowl, add the coconut sugar and yeast, and stir. Let rest for 5 minutes.

3. Preheat the oven to 170°F. Once the oven is hot, turn it off.

4. Add the applesauce, coconut oil, vanilla, lemon zest, nutmeg, and 2 cups of flour to the yeast mixture. Using a large wooden spoon, mix for 3 to 4 minutes before adding 2 more cups of flour and mixing for another 2 to 3 minutes. If the dough is quite sticky, add the remaining ½ cup of flour.

5. Transfer the dough to a lightly floured surface and knead for about 5 minutes, or until it forms a soft ball. Lightly grease a large bowl and place the dough in it. Cover with a clean kitchen towel and place in the oven (with the door slightly open) for 30 to 60 minutes, until doubled in size. While the dough is rising, line two large baking sheets with parchment paper.

6. Once the dough has doubled in size, punch it down, place it on a lightly floured surface, and roll it into a rectangle about ½ inch thick. Use a large biscuit cutter to cut out 16 donuts. Transfer to the prepared baking sheets, cover with a clean kitchen towel, and let rest for 15 minutes.

7. While the donuts are resting, preheat the oven to 350°F.

8. Bake for 12 to 15 minutes, until puffy and lightly golden on top. Let cool completely.

9. **To make the chocolate glaze:** While the donuts are cooling, in a medium bowl, combine the powdered sugar, cocoa powder, vanilla, and 3 tablespoons of milk. Whisk to form a thick but pourable glaze, adding the remaining 1 tablespoon of milk if needed.

10. Once the donuts have cooled, make a slit from one side of each donut through to the center by inserting a 1-inch-wide knife blade. Insert the piping nozzle into the slit and gently pipe in the filling. Dip the top of each donut in the chocolate glaze or spoon the glaze over the tops.

PER DONUT: Calories: 276; Total fat: 7g; Saturated fat: 6g; Cholesterol: 0g; Sodium: 15mg; Carbohydrates: 47g; Fiber: 2g; Sugar: 16g; Protein: 5g

BLACKBERRY-BASIL-RICOTTA DONUTS

PREP TIME: 30 minutes, plus 1 hour 15 minutes for the dough to rise
COOK TIME: 15 minutes
MAKES 16 DONUTS

Blackberry and basil are an amazing combination, and I'm a huge fan of using it everywhere—including in a donut. Both Tofutti and Kite Hill make excellent vegan versions of ricotta, and I highly recommend using them. If you have leftover ricotta filling, serve it on toasted baguettes for breakfast or lunch. It's a delicious spread!

FOR THE RICOTTA FILLING

2 cups vegan ricotta
2 tablespoons blackberry jam
4 to 6 fresh basil leaves, finely chopped

FOR THE DONUTS

1¼ cups unsweetened nondairy milk
¼ cup (50 grams) coconut sugar
1 (¼-ounce) packet active dry yeast
½ cup unsweetened applesauce, at room temperature
¼ cup coconut oil, melted
1 teaspoon vanilla extract
1 teaspoon grated lemon zest
¼ teaspoon ground nutmeg
4½ cups (540 grams) all-purpose flour

FOR THE GLAZE

2 cups (227 grams) powdered sugar
¼ cup unsweetened nondairy milk
2 tablespoons blackberry jam
1 teaspoon vanilla extract
⅛ teaspoon salt

1. **To make the ricotta filling:** In a large bowl, combine the ricotta, blackberry jam, and basil and mix until well combined. Transfer to a pastry bag fitted with a cream piping nozzle and refrigerate until needed.

2. **To make the donuts:** In a small microwave-safe bowl, microwave the milk for 1 minute, or until steaming but not scalding or boiling. Transfer to a large bowl, add the coconut sugar and yeast, and stir. Let rest for 5 minutes.

3. Preheat the oven to 170°F. Once the oven is hot, turn it off.

4. Add the applesauce, coconut oil, vanilla, lemon zest, nutmeg, and 2 cups of flour to the yeast mixture. Using a large wooden spoon, mix for 3 to 4 minutes before adding 2 more cups of flour and mixing for another 2 to 3 minutes. If the dough is quite sticky, add the remaining ½ cup of flour.

5. Transfer the dough to a lightly floured surface and knead for about 5 minutes, or until it forms a soft ball. Lightly grease a large bowl and place the dough in it. Cover with a clean kitchen towel and place in the oven (with the door slightly open) for 30 to 60 minutes, until doubled in size. While the dough is rising, line two large baking sheets with parchment paper.

6. Once the dough has doubled in size, punch it down, place it on a lightly floured surface, and roll it into a rectangle about ½ inch thick. Use a large biscuit cutter to cut out 16 donuts. Transfer to the prepared baking sheets, cover with a clean kitchen towel, and let rest for 15 minutes.

7. While the donuts are resting, preheat the oven to 350°F.

8. Bake for 12 to 15 minutes, until puffy and lightly golden on top. Let cool.

9. **To make the glaze:** In a medium saucepan, combine the powdered sugar, milk, blackberry jam, vanilla, and salt over medium heat. Cook, whisking continuously, until combined, then remove from the heat.

10. Once the donuts have cooled, make a slit from one side of each donut right through to the center by inserting a 1-inch-wide knife blade. Insert the piping nozzle into the slit and gently pipe in the ricotta filling. Dip the top of each donut into the glaze or spoon the glaze directly onto the donut.

PER DONUT: Calories: 296; Total fat: 8g; Saturated fat: 5g; Cholesterol: 0g; Sodium: 108mg; Carbohydrates: 52g; Fiber: 1g; Sugar: 19g; Protein: 5g

LEMON MERINGUE DONUTS

PREP TIME: 45 minutes, plus 1 hour 15 minutes for the dough to rise
COOK TIME: 25 minutes

MAKES 16 DONUTS

If Boston cream pie can become a donut, why can't lemon meringue? We're going to take a classic lemon-filled donut and elevate it with the addition of a real eggless meringue topping. Most store-bought lemon curds use eggs, so I've included my go-to homemade vegan version. Save this lemon curd recipe—it's delicious in so many desserts.

FOR THE LEMON CURD FILLING

1½ cups (300 grams) granulated sugar
1¼ cups full-fat coconut milk
¾ cup freshly squeezed lemon juice
  (from 4 to 5 lemons)

6 tablespoons (42 grams) cornstarch
2 teaspoons grated lemon zest

FOR THE DONUTS

1¼ cups unsweetened nondairy milk
¼ cup (50 grams) granulated sugar
1 (¼-ounce) packet active dry yeast
½ cup unsweetened applesauce, at
  room temperature

¼ cup coconut oil, melted
1 teaspoon vanilla extract
1 teaspoon grated lemon zest
¼ teaspoon ground nutmeg
4½ cups (540 grams) all-purpose flour

FOR THE MERINGUE TOPPING

3 ounces aquafaba (brine from 1 can
  of chickpeas)
½ teaspoon cream of tartar

¾ cup (150 grams) granulated sugar
½ teaspoon vanilla extract

1. **To make the lemon curd filling:** In a medium saucepan, heat the sugar, coconut milk, lemon juice, cornstarch, and lemon zest over medium heat. Whisk well to ensure the cornstarch is fully dissolved and cook, stirring constantly, for about 7 minutes, or until the mixture has thickened into a curd-like consistency. Remove from the heat and cool completely before transferring to a pastry bag fitted with a cream piping nozzle.

2. **To make the donuts:** In a small microwave-safe bowl, microwave the milk for 1 minute, or until steaming but not scalding or boiling. Transfer to a large bowl, add the sugar and yeast, and stir. Let rest for 5 minutes.

3. Preheat the oven to 170°F. Once the oven is hot, turn it off.

4. Add the applesauce, coconut oil, vanilla, lemon zest, nutmeg, and 2 cups of flour to the yeast mixture. Using a large wooden spoon, mix for 3 to 4 minutes before adding 2 more cups of flour and mixing for another 2 to 3 minutes. If the dough is quite sticky, add the remaining ½ cup of flour.

5. Transfer the dough to a lightly floured surface and knead for about 5 minutes, or until it forms a soft ball. Lightly grease a large bowl and place the dough in it. Cover with a clean kitchen towel and place in the oven (with the door slightly open) for 30 to 60 minutes, until doubled in size. While the dough is rising, line two large baking sheets with parchment paper and set aside.

6. Once the dough has doubled in size, punch it down, place it on a lightly floured surface, and roll it into a rectangle about ½ inch thick. Use a large biscuit cutter (or a round cookie cutter about 5 inches in diameter) to cut out 16 donuts. Transfer to the prepared baking sheets, cover with a clean kitchen towel, and let rest for 15 minutes.

7. While the donuts are resting, preheat the oven to 350°F.

8. Bake for 12 to 15 minutes, or until puffy and lightly golden on top. Let cool completely.

CONTINUED ▷

9. **To make the meringue topping:** While the donuts are cooling, preheat the broiler to low.

10. In a large bowl, using a handheld electric mixer on medium-high speed, whisk the aquafaba and cream of tartar for at least 6 minutes, or until soft peaks form.

11. Gradually add the granulated sugar, 1 tablespoon at a time, as you continue beating for 15 to 20 minutes, until stiff peaks form and the meringue has a glossy shine to it. Add the vanilla and beat for 1 to 2 minutes.

12. Once the donuts have cooled, make a slit from one side of each donut right through to the center by inserting a 1-inch-wide knife blade. Insert the piping nozzle into the slit and gently pipe in the lemon curd. Scoop a heaping tablespoon of meringue on top of each donut, and place back on the baking sheets. Place one baking sheet of donuts on the top oven rack and, keeping the oven door slightly open, very lightly brown the meringue peaks for 1 to 2 minutes. Repeat with the remaining baking sheet of donuts.

INGREDIENT TIP: Just like egg white meringue, aquafaba meringue can be finicky. To ensure the best results with your meringue, use a metal bowl if possible and chill it for 15 to 20 minutes in the freezer before starting. Also ensure your bowl is clean and dry, as moisture in the bowl (other than the aquafaba) can keep the meringue from whipping properly.

PER DONUT: Calories: 339; Total fat: 8g; Saturated fat: 6g; Cholesterol: 0g; Sodium: 13mg; Carbohydrates: 64g; Fiber: 1g; Sugar: 33g; Protein: 5g

STUFFED S'MORES DONUTS

PREP TIME: 25 minutes, plus 1 hour 15 minutes for the dough to rise
COOK TIME: 15 minutes
LOW REFINED SUGAR OPTION
MAKES 16 DONUTS

One of the best things about summer for me is making s'mores over an open fire at my cottage. I've recreated that iconic summer dessert in donut form—complete with a homemade marshmallow creme filling that takes mere minutes to make. To really get that campfire feeling, use a small kitchen blowtorch to "roast" the marshmallows on top.

FOR THE MARSHMALLOW CREME
3 ounces aquafaba (brine from 1 can of chickpeas)
2 teaspoons vanilla extract
½ teaspoon cream of tartar
¾ cup (150 grams) granulated sugar
3 tablespoons powdered sugar

FOR THE DONUTS
1¼ cups unsweetened nondairy milk
¼ cup (50 grams) granulated sugar
1 (¼-ounce) packet active dry yeast
½ cup unsweetened applesauce, at room temperature
¼ cup coconut oil, melted
1 teaspoon vanilla extract
1 teaspoon grated lemon zest
¼ teaspoon ground nutmeg
4½ cups (540 grams) all-purpose flour

FOR THE CHOCOLATE GLAZE
1 cup (113 grams) powdered sugar
3 tablespoons dark cocoa powder
½ teaspoon vanilla extract
4 tablespoons unsweetened nondairy milk

CONTINUED ▶

1. **To make the marshmallow creme:** In a large bowl, using a handheld electric mixer on medium-high speed, whisk the aquafaba, vanilla, and cream of tartar for 8 to 10 minutes, until the mixture forms stiff peaks. If you can turn the bowl upside down and the mixture doesn't fall out, you've hit the stiff-peak stage. Slowly add the granulated sugar and powdered sugar and continue beating until all the sugar is dissolved and the fluff has a glossy shine to it. Transfer to a pastry bag fitted with a cream piping nozzle and set aside until needed.

2. **To make the donuts:** In a microwave-safe bowl, microwave the milk for 1 minute, or until steaming but not scalding or boiling. Transfer it to a large bowl, add the sugar and yeast, and stir. Let rest for 5 minutes, or until a bit frothy.

3. Preheat the oven to 170°F. Once the oven is hot, turn it off.

4. Add the applesauce, coconut oil, vanilla, lemon zest, nutmeg, and 2 cups of flour to the yeast mixture. Using a large wooden spoon, mix for 3 to 4 minutes before adding 2 more cups of flour and mixing for another 2 to 3 minutes. If the dough is quite sticky, add the remaining ½ cup of flour.

5. Transfer the dough to a lightly floured surface and knead for about 5 minutes, or until it forms a soft ball. Lightly grease a large bowl and place the dough in it. Cover with a clean kitchen towel and place in the oven (with the door slightly open) for 30 to 60 minutes, until doubled in size. While the dough is rising, line two large baking sheets with parchment paper and set aside.

6. Once the dough has doubled in size, punch it down, place it on a lightly floured surface, and roll it into a rectangle about ½ inch thick. Use a large biscuit cutter (or a round cookie cutter about 5 inches in diameter) to cut out 16 donuts. Transfer to the prepared baking sheets, cover with a clean kitchen towel, and let rest for 15 minutes.

7. While the donuts are resting, preheat the oven to 350°F.

8. Bake for 12 to 15 minutes, or until puffy and lightly golden on top. Let cool completely.

9. **To make the chocolate glaze:** While the donuts are cooling, in a medium bowl, combine the powdered sugar, cocoa powder, vanilla, and 3 tablespoons of milk. Whisk to form a thick but pourable glaze, adding the remaining 1 tablespoon of milk if needed.

10. Once the donuts have cooled, make a slit from one side of each donut through to the center by inserting a 1-inch-wide knife blade. Insert the piping nozzle into the slit and gently pipe in the marshmallow creme. Dip the top of each donut in the chocolate glaze or spoon the glaze over the tops.

LIGHTEN UP TIP: Try swapping out the granulated sugar in the donut dough for coconut sugar. Coconut sugar is not refined and has a much lower glycemic index.

PER DONUT: Calories: 253; Total fat: 4g; Saturated fat: 3g; Cholesterol: 0g; Sodium: 12mg; Carbohydrates: 50g; Fiber: 2g; Sugar: 22g; Protein: 5g

RASPBERRY-MANGO DONUTS

PREP TIME: 50 minutes, plus 3 hours 15 minutes for
the dough to rise and the curd to chill COOK TIME: 15 minutes

LOW REFINED SUGAR

MAKES 16 DONUTS

Tart raspberry and sweet mango work so well with rich cream cheese in this fluffy yeast donut. I used homemade mango curd, but you could also use store-bought mango puree to save time.

FOR THE MANGO CURD

4 cups frozen mango, thawed

1 cup full-fat coconut milk

½ cup (100 grams) superfine
  or caster sugar

2 tablespoons cornstarch

Juice of 1½ limes

⅛ teaspoon salt

2 tablespoons coconut oil

FOR THE FILLING

2 cups plain vegan cream cheese,
  at room temperature

2 tablespoons seedless raspberry jam

FOR THE DONUTS

1¼ cups unsweetened nondairy milk

¼ cup (50 grams) coconut sugar

1 (¼-ounce) packet active dry yeast

½ cup unsweetened applesauce, at
  room temperature

¼ cup coconut oil, melted

1 teaspoon vanilla extract

1 teaspoon grated lemon zest

¼ teaspoon ground nutmeg

4½ cups (540 grams) all-purpose flour

1. **To make the mango curd:** In a blender or food processor, combine the mango, coconut milk, superfine sugar, cornstarch, lime juice, and salt. Process until smooth, then strain through a fine mesh strainer into a small saucepan. Place the pan over medium-low heat and bring to a low boil, stirring constantly. Once the mixture is boiling, remove from the heat and stir in the coconut oil. Transfer to a bowl and chill in the refrigerator for 1 to 2 hours.

2. **To make the filling:** In a large bowl, combine the cream cheese and raspberry jam and mix well. Transfer to a pastry bag fitted with a narrow tip and refrigerate until needed.

3. **To make the donuts:** In a small microwave-safe bowl, microwave the milk for 1 minute, or until steaming but not scalding or boiling. Transfer to a large bowl, add the coconut sugar and yeast, and stir. Let rest for 5 minutes.

4. Preheat the oven to 170°F. Once the oven is hot, turn it off.

5. Add the applesauce, coconut oil, vanilla, lemon zest, nutmeg, and 2 cups of flour to the yeast mixture. Using a large wooden spoon, mix for 3 to 4 minutes before adding 2 more cups of flour and mixing for another 2 to 3 minutes. If the dough is quite sticky, add the remaining ½ cup of flour.

6. Transfer the dough to a lightly floured surface and knead for about 5 minutes, or until it forms a soft ball. Lightly grease a large bowl and place the dough in it. Cover with a clean kitchen towel and place in the oven (with the door slightly open) for 30 to 60 minutes, until doubled in size. While the dough is rising, line two large baking sheets with parchment paper.

7. Once the dough has doubled in size, punch it down, place it on a lightly floured surface, and roll it into a rectangle about ½ inch thick. Use a large biscuit cutter (or a round cookie cutter about 5 inches in diameter) to cut out 16 donuts. Transfer to the prepared baking sheets, cover with a clean kitchen towel, and let rest for 15 minutes.

8. While the donuts are resting, preheat the oven to 350°F.

9. Bake for 12 to 15 minutes, or until puffy and lightly golden on top. Let cool completely.

10. Once the donuts have cooled, scoop out a well in the top of each donut to the center, about 3 inches in diameter. Pipe the cream cheese filling into the hole, then drizzle the mango curd on top.

PER DONUT: Calories: 361; Total fat: 17g; Saturated fat: 12g; Cholesterol: 0g; Sodium: 164mg; Carbohydrates: 45g; Fiber: 2g; Sugar: 16g; Protein: 7g

STRAWBERRY JELLY DONUTS

PREP TIME: 30 minutes, plus 1 hour 15 minutes for the dough to rise
COOK TIME: 15 minutes

MAKES 16 DONUTS

A donut book wouldn't be complete without a recipe for the classic donut-shop strawberry-filled donut, so . . . here it is! I like to brush my donuts with melted butter and roll them in granulated sugar, but you could also toss them in powdered sugar if you prefer. Just skip the brush of butter, as it will cause the powdered sugar to melt.

1¼ cups unsweetened nondairy milk
¾ cup (150 grams) granulated sugar, divided
1 (¼-ounce) packet active dry yeast
½ cup unsweetened applesauce, at room temperature
¼ cup coconut oil, melted

1 teaspoon vanilla extract
1 teaspoon grated lemon zest
¼ teaspoon ground nutmeg
4½ cups (540 grams) all-purpose flour
½ cup seedless strawberry jelly, like Smucker's
3 tablespoons vegan butter, melted

1. In a small microwave-safe bowl, microwave the milk for 1 minute, or until steaming but not scalding or boiling. Transfer it to a large bowl, add ¼ cup of sugar and the yeast, and stir to combine. Let rest for 5 minutes, or until a bit frothy.

2. Preheat the oven to 170°F. Once the oven is hot, turn it off.

3. Add the applesauce, coconut oil, vanilla, lemon zest, nutmeg, and 2 cups of flour to the yeast mixture. Using a large wooden spoon, mix for 3 to 4 minutes before adding 2 more cups of flour and mixing for another 2 to 3 minutes. If the dough is quite sticky, add the remaining ½ cup of flour.

4. Transfer the dough to a lightly floured surface and knead for about 5 minutes, or until it forms a soft ball. Lightly grease a large bowl and place the dough in it. Cover with a clean kitchen towel and place in the oven (with the door slightly open) for 30 to 60 minutes, until doubled in size. While the dough is rising, line two large baking sheets with parchment paper and set aside.

5. Once the dough has doubled in size, punch it down, place it on a lightly floured surface, and roll it into a rectangle about ½ inch thick. Use a large biscuit cutter (or a round cookie cutter about 5 inches in diameter) to cut out 16 donuts. Transfer to the prepared baking sheets, cover with a clean kitchen towel, and let rest for 15 minutes.

6. While the donuts are resting, preheat the oven to 350°F.

7. Bake for 12 to 15 minutes, or until puffy and lightly golden on top. Let cool completely.

8. While the donuts are cooling, spoon the jelly into a pastry bag fitted with a cream piping nozzle and place the remaining ½ cup of sugar onto a rimmed plate.

9. Once the donuts have cooled, make a slit from one side of each donut right through to the center by inserting a 1-inch-wide knife blade. Insert the piping nozzle. Gently fill each donut with the jelly. Brush the donuts with the melted butter and roll them in the sugar.

INGREDIENT TIP: For best results when piping, use a strawberry jelly instead of jam. Jelly is similar to jam but doesn't contain any pieces of fruit, which can "jam up" the pastry bag (pardon the pun), making it difficult to fill the donuts.

PER DONUT: Calories: 252; Total fat: 6g; Saturated fat: 3g; Cholesterol: 0g; Sodium: 14mg; Carbohydrates: 45g; Fiber: 1g; Sugar: 16g; Protein: 4g

CARAMEL APPLE PIE DONUTS

PREP TIME: 20 minutes, plus 1 hour 15 minutes for the dough to rise
COOK TIME: 30 minutes
LOW REFINED SUGAR OPTION
MAKES 16 DONUTS

This donut delivers big apple flavor thanks to the homemade caramel apple pie filling. I like to double the filling recipe and freeze half of it to use another time or in different desserts (hint: It makes a great topping for ice cream sundaes!). Thaw it overnight in the refrigerator before using for best results.

FOR THE APPLE PIE FILLING

3 medium Granny Smith apples, finely diced (about 2 cups)
1 tablespoon freshly squeezed lemon juice
¼ cup (50 grams) granulated sugar
¼ cup (53 grams) lightly packed brown sugar

¼ cup (28 grams) cornstarch
½ teaspoon ground cinnamon
⅛ teaspoon ground nutmeg
1 cup water
½ cup unsweetened apple juice
2 teaspoons vegan butter, cold

FOR THE DONUTS

1¼ cups unsweetened nondairy milk
¼ cup (50 grams) coconut sugar
1 (¼-ounce) packet active dry yeast
½ cup unsweetened applesauce, at room temperature

¼ cup coconut oil, melted
1 teaspoon vanilla extract
½ teaspoon ground cinnamon
4½ cups (540 grams) all-purpose flour

FOR THE CINNAMON-SUGAR TOPPING

¼ cup granulated sugar
2 teaspoons ground cinnamon

4 tablespoons (½ stick) vegan butter, melted

1. **To make the apple pie filling:** In a large bowl, combine the apples and lemon juice. Set aside.

2. In a wide saucepan, combine the granulated sugar, brown sugar, cornstarch, cinnamon, and nutmeg. Add the water and apple juice and mix. Bring it to a boil, then reduce the heat to medium, add the apples, and cook for about 10 minutes, or until the apples are soft and the sauce has thickened. Remove from the heat and add the butter, stirring until incorporated. Let cool at room temperature for 1 hour.

3. **To make the donuts:** While the apple pie filling is cooling, in a microwave-safe bowl, microwave the milk for 1 minute, or until steaming but not scalding or boiling. Transfer to a large bowl, add the coconut sugar and yeast, and stir. Let rest for 5 minutes, or until a bit frothy.

4. Preheat the oven to 170°F. Once the oven is hot, turn it off.

5. Add the applesauce, coconut oil, vanilla, cinnamon, and 2 cups of flour to the yeast mixture. Using a large wooden spoon, mix for 3 to 4 minutes before adding 2 more cups of flour and mixing for another 2 to 3 minutes. If the dough is quite sticky, add the remaining ½ cup of flour.

6. Transfer the dough to a lightly floured surface and knead for about 5 minutes, or until it forms a soft ball. Lightly grease a large bowl and place the dough in it. Cover with a clean kitchen towel and place in the oven (with the door slightly open) for 30 to 60 minutes, until doubled in size. While the dough is rising, line two large baking sheets with parchment paper and set aside.

7. Once the dough has doubled in size, punch it down, place it on a lightly floured surface, and roll it into a rectangle about ½ inch thick. Use a large biscuit cutter (or a round cookie cutter about 5 inches in diameter) to cut out 16 donuts. Transfer to the prepared baking sheets, cover with a clean kitchen towel, and let rest for 15 minutes.

8. While the donuts are resting, preheat the oven to 350°F.

9. Bake for 12 to 15 minutes, or until puffy and lightly golden on top. Let cool completely.

CONTINUED ▶

10. **To make the cinnamon-sugar topping:** While the donuts are cooling, on a rimmed plate, mix together the sugar and cinnamon.

11. Once the donuts have cooled, brush the donuts with the melted butter and toss them in the cinnamon sugar, then scoop out a well in the top of each donut to the center, about 3 inches in diameter, and spoon the apple pie filling into the hole.

LIGHTEN UP TIP: Lower the sugar content of this donut by skipping the cinnamon-sugar coating, and consider using monk fruit sweetener in place of granulated sugar in the apple pie filling. Use 2 tablespoons of monk fruit sweetener to replace the ¼ cup of granulated sugar. You can also swap out the brown sugar for raw coconut sugar or maple syrup.

PER DONUT: Calories: 278; Total fat: 7g; Saturated fat: 4g; Cholesterol: 0g; Sodium: 14mg; Carbohydrates: 49g; Fiber: 2g; Sugar: 18g; Protein: 4g

PEACH STREUSEL DONUTS

PREP TIME: 10 minutes, plus 15 minutes to chill the streusel and
1 hour 15 minutes for the dough to rise • COOK TIME: 30 minutes
MAKES 16 DONUTS

Peach season is my favorite, and I'm obsessed with making peach desserts,
like these peach streusel donuts. They capture the essence of a freshly
baked peach crisp in a fluffy yeast donut. The streusel doesn't take long
to make, but it can also be prepared up to two days ahead of time to
shorten your prep time on bake day.

FOR THE STREUSEL

1 cup (120 grams) all-purpose flour
½ cup (106 grams) lightly packed
   brown sugar
¼ cup (50 grams) granulated sugar

½ teaspoon ground cinnamon
¼ teaspoon salt
6 tablespoons (¾ stick) vegan butter,
   cold, diced

FOR THE DONUTS

1¼ cups unsweetened nondairy milk
¼ cup (50 grams) coconut sugar
1 (¼-ounce) packet active dry yeast
½ cup unsweetened applesauce, at
   room temperature

¼ cup coconut oil, melted
1 teaspoon vanilla extract
½ teaspoon ground cinnamon
4½ cups (540 grams) all-purpose flour

FOR THE GLAZE

½ cup powdered sugar
1 to 2 tablespoons unsweetened plain
   or vanilla nondairy milk
½ teaspoon vanilla extract

½ teaspoon ground cinnamon
2 large peaches, diced

CONTINUED ▷

1. **To make the streusel:** Preheat the oven to 350°F and line a sheet pan with parchment paper.

2. In a small bowl, combine the flour, brown sugar, granulated sugar, cinnamon, and salt. Use a fork or a pastry cutter to cut the butter into the flour mixture until it resembles small peas. Place the bowl in the freezer and chill for 15 minutes.

3. Transfer the chilled streusel to the prepared baking sheet and bake for 10 to 12 minutes. Let the streusel and the oven cool completely.

4. **To make the donuts:** In a microwave-safe bowl, microwave the milk for 1 minute, or until steaming but not scalding or boiling. Transfer to a large bowl, add the coconut sugar and yeast, and stir to combine. Let rest for 5 minutes, or until a bit frothy.

5. Preheat the oven to 170°F. Once the oven is hot, turn it off.

6. Add the applesauce, coconut oil, vanilla, cinnamon, and 2 cups of flour to the yeast mixture. Using a large wooden spoon, mix for 3 to 4 minutes before adding 2 more cups of flour and mixing for another 2 to 3 minutes. If the dough is quite sticky, add the remaining ½ cup of flour.

7. Transfer the dough to a lightly floured surface and knead for about 5 minutes, or until it forms a soft ball. Lightly grease a large bowl and place the dough in it. Cover with a clean kitchen towel and place in the oven (with the door slightly open) for 30 to 60 minutes, until doubled in size. While the dough is rising, line two large baking sheets with parchment paper and set aside.

8. Once the dough has doubled in size, punch it down, place it on a lightly floured surface, and roll it into a rectangle about ½ inch thick. Use a large biscuit cutter (or a round cookie cutter about 5 inches in diameter) to cut out 16 donuts. Transfer to the prepared baking sheets, cover with a clean kitchen towel, and let rest for 15 minutes.

9. While the donuts are resting, preheat the oven to 350°F.

10. Bake for 12 to 15 minutes, or until puffy and lightly golden on top. Let cool completely.

11. **To make the glaze:** While the donuts are cooling, in a small bowl, combine the powdered sugar, milk, vanilla, and cinnamon and whisk until a thick but pourable glaze forms. Transfer the streusel to a large bowl, breaking up any large chunks, and combine with the diced peaches.

12. Once the donuts have cooled, scoop out a well in the top of each donut to the center, about 3 inches in diameter, spoon the peach streusel filling into the hole, and drizzle with the glaze.

VARIATION TIP: Switch up the fruit in this recipe for more seasonal flavors. Cherry, blueberry, raspberry, and apple all work well if it's not peach season.

PER DONUT: Calories: 307; Total fat: 8g; Saturated fat: 4g; Cholesterol: 0g; Sodium: 51mg; Carbohydrates: 53g; Fiber: 2g; Sugar: 19g; Protein: 5g

COOKIES AND CREAM DONUTS

PREP TIME: 25 minutes, plus 1 hour 15 minutes for the dough to rise
COOK TIME: 15 minutes
MAKES 16 DONUTS

Channel your inner kid and treat yourself to these chocolate yeast donuts filled with buttercream made with everyone's favorite sandwich cookie. I've added dark cocoa powder to the yeasted dough to give the donuts a deep chocolate flavor that pairs well with the rich, cookie-studded cream filling.

FOR THE DONUTS
1¼ cups unsweetened nondairy milk
¼ cup (50 grams) coconut sugar
1 (¼-ounce) packet active dry yeast
½ cup unsweetened applesauce, at room temperature

½ cup (42 grams) dark cocoa powder
¼ cup coconut oil, melted
1 teaspoon vanilla extract
½ teaspoon ground cinnamon
4 cups (480 grams) all-purpose flour

FOR THE BUTTERCREAM FILLING
10 sandwich cookies, such as Oreos
3 cups (340 grams) powdered sugar
1 cup (2 sticks) vegan butter, at room temperature

2 tablespoons unsweetened nondairy milk
1 teaspoon vanilla extract

FOR THE VANILLA GLAZE
2 cups powdered sugar
⅓ to ½ cup unsweetened plain or vanilla nondairy milk

1 teaspoon vanilla extract
10 sandwich cookies, chopped into large chunks

1. **To make the donuts:** In a microwave-safe bowl, microwave the milk for 1 minute, or until steaming but not scalding or boiling. Transfer to a large bowl, add the coconut sugar and yeast, and stir to combine. Let rest for 5 minutes, or until a bit frothy.

2. Preheat the oven to 170°F. Once the oven is hot, turn it off.

3. Add the applesauce, cocoa powder, coconut oil, vanilla, cinnamon, and 2 cups of flour to the yeast mixture. Using a large wooden spoon, mix for 3 to 4 minutes before adding the remaining 2 cups of flour and mixing for another 2 to 3 minutes.

4. Transfer the dough to a lightly floured surface and knead for about 5 minutes, or until it forms a soft ball. Lightly grease a large bowl and place the dough in it. Cover with a clean kitchen towel and place in the oven (with the door slightly open) for 30 to 60 minutes, until doubled in size. While the dough is rising, line two large baking sheets with parchment paper and set aside.

5. Once the dough has doubled in size, punch it down, place it on a lightly floured surface, and roll it into a rectangle about ½ inch thick. Use a large biscuit cutter to cut out 16 donuts. Transfer to the prepared baking sheets, cover with a clean kitchen towel, and let rest for 15 minutes.

6. While the donuts are resting, preheat the oven to 350°F.

7. Bake for 12 to 15 minutes, or until puffy and lightly golden on top. Let cool.

8. **To make the buttercream filling:** While the donuts are cooling, in a food processor, crush the sandwich cookies into a powder (alternatively, you could do this by placing them in a resealable bag and crushing them with a rolling pin). Add the powdered sugar, butter, milk, and vanilla and pulse until buttercream frosting forms. If you don't have a food processor, use an electric hand mixer on medium speed to whip the buttercream. Transfer to a pastry bag fitted with a wide, round tip and set aside.

9. **To make the vanilla glaze:** In a small bowl, combine the powdered sugar, milk, and vanilla and whisk until a thick but pourable glaze forms.

10. Once the donuts have cooled, make a slit from one side right through to the center of each donut by inserting a 1-inch-wide knife blade. Gently fill each donut with the buttercream filling, then dip the tops in the glaze and garnish with the chopped cookies.

PER DONUT: Calories: 469; Total fat: 19g; Saturated fat: 6g; Cholesterol: 0g; Sodium: 77mg; Carbohydrates: 73g; Fiber: 2g; Sugar: 41g; Protein: 5g

COCONUT CUSTARD DONUTS

PREP TIME: 35 minutes, plus 1 hour 15 minutes for the dough to rise
COOK TIME: 30 minutes
MAKES 16 DONUTS

In my pre-vegan days, there was a bakery near my office that made the best coconut custard donuts. I still miss those donuts, so I turned my Boston cream filling into a coconut cream and created my own version.

FOR THE CUSTARD FILLING

2 cups full-fat coconut milk
½ cup maple syrup
¼ cup cornstarch

1 tablespoon coconut extract
⅛ teaspoon ground turmeric (for color)

FOR THE DONUTS

1¼ cups unsweetened nondairy milk
¼ cup (50 grams) coconut sugar
1 (¼-ounce) packet active dry yeast
½ cup unsweetened applesauce, at room temperature

¼ cup coconut oil, melted
1 teaspoon vanilla extract
½ teaspoon ground cinnamon
4½ cups (540 grams) all-purpose flour

FOR THE GLAZE

½ cup (42 grams) coconut flakes
3 cups (340 grams) powdered sugar
4 tablespoons coconut milk

1½ tablespoons coconut oil, melted
1 teaspoon vanilla extract

1. **To make the custard filling:** In a medium saucepan, simmer the coconut milk, maple syrup, cornstarch, coconut extract, and turmeric over medium heat, whisking constantly, for 6 to 8 minutes, until thickened. Remove from the heat and let cool completely. Once the filling has cooled, transfer it to a pastry bag fitted with a cream piping nozzle and refrigerate until needed.

2. **To make the donuts:** In a microwave-safe bowl, microwave the milk for 1 minute, or until steaming but not scalding or boiling. Transfer to a large bowl, add the coconut sugar and yeast, and stir. Let rest for 5 minutes, or until a bit frothy.

3. Preheat the oven to 170°F. Once the oven is hot, turn it off.

4. Add the applesauce, coconut oil, vanilla, cinnamon, and 2 cups of flour to the yeast mixture. Using a large wooden spoon, mix for 3 to 4 minutes before adding 2 more cups of flour and mixing for another 2 to 3 minutes. If the dough is quite sticky, add the remaining ½ cup of flour.

5. Transfer the dough to a lightly floured surface and knead for about 5 minutes, or until it forms a soft ball. Lightly grease a large bowl and place the dough in it. Cover with a clean kitchen towel and place in the oven (with the door slightly open) for 30 to 60 minutes, until doubled in size. While the dough is rising, line two large baking sheets with parchment paper and set aside.

6. Once the dough has doubled in size, punch it down, place it on a lightly floured surface, and roll it into a rectangle about ½ inch thick. Use a large biscuit cutter (or a round cookie cutter about 5 inches in diameter) to cut out 16 donuts. Transfer to the prepared baking sheets, cover with a clean kitchen towel, and let rest for 15 minutes.

7. While the donuts are resting, preheat the oven to 350°F.

8. Bake for 12 to 15 minutes, or until puffy and lightly golden on top. Let cool completely.

9. **To make the glaze:** While the donuts are cooling, in a wide skillet, toast the coconut flakes, stirring constantly, for about 5 minutes, or until lightly browned. Transfer to a bowl to cool. Then, in a medium bowl, combine the powdered sugar, 3 tablespoons of coconut milk, the coconut oil, and vanilla. Whisk to form a thick but pourable glaze, adding the remaining 1 tablespoon of coconut milk if needed.

10. Once the donuts have cooled, make a slit in one side right through to the center of each donut by inserting a 1-inch-wide knife blade. Insert the piping nozzle into the slit and gently pipe in the custard filling. Dip the top of each filled donut in the glaze and sprinkle with the toasted coconut flakes.

PER DONUT: Calories: 371; Total fat: 13g; Saturated fat: 10g; Cholesterol: 0g; Sodium: 17mg; Carbohydrates: 60g; Fiber: 2g; Sugar: 29g; Protein: 5g

**Cornbread Queso
Donuts, page 110**

CHAPTER 5

SAVORY DONUTS

Caramelized-Onion-Stuffed
Everything Bagel Donuts **102**

Sun-Dried Tomato and Basil Donuts **105**

Cranberry Stuffing Donuts **106**

Black Olive and Jalapeño Donuts **108**

Savory "Cheese" and Herb Donuts **109**

Cornbread Queso Donuts **110**

Scallion and Smoked "Gouda" Donuts **112**

CARAMELIZED-ONION-STUFFED EVERYTHING BAGEL DONUTS

PREP TIME: 25 minutes, plus 1 hour 15 minutes for the dough to rise
COOK TIME: 55 minutes
LOW REFINED SUGAR
MAKES 16 DONUTS

These savory stuffed donuts might just be my new favorite breakfast. With a caramelized-onion cream cheese filling and a generous helping of everything bagel seasoning, they are the perfect replacement for your morning bagel. I like to use Trader Joe's Everything but the Bagel seasoning, but any brand will work just as well.

FOR THE CARAMELIZED ONION FILLING
¼ cup grapeseed or other neutral oil
2 tablespoons vegan butter
3 or 4 large onions, sliced
¼ cup water or vegetable broth
½ teaspoon kosher salt
2 (8-ounce) packages vegan cream cheese, at room temperature

FOR THE DONUTS
1¼ cups unsweetened nondairy milk
¼ cup (50 grams) granulated sugar
1 (¼-ounce) packet active dry yeast
½ cup unsweetened applesauce, at room temperature
4 tablespoons (½ stick) vegan butter, melted
2 teaspoons dried minced onion
1 teaspoon onion powder
1 teaspoon garlic powder
½ teaspoon salt
4½ cups (540 grams) all-purpose flour

FOR THE CREAM CHEESE TOPPING
1 (8-ounce) package vegan cream cheese, at room temperature
3 tablespoons everything bagel seasoning, plus more for garnish, if desired

1. **To make the caramelized onion filling:** In a Dutch oven or heavy-bottomed stainless steel pan, melt the grapeseed oil and butter together over medium heat. Add the onions and cook, stirring every few minutes and scraping up any dark bits that form on the bottom of the pan, for 30 to 40 minutes, until the onions are golden and smell sweet and caramelized.

2. Once the onions have caramelized, add the water and stir as it bubbles, scraping up any bits on the bottom of the pan. Remove from the heat and add the salt. Transfer to a bowl and chill in the refrigerator for 30 minutes. Add the cream cheese and mix well. Store in the refrigerator until needed.

3. **To make the donuts:** In a microwave-safe bowl, microwave the milk for 1 minute, or until steaming but not scalding or boiling. Transfer to a large bowl, add the sugar and yeast, and stir to combine. Let it rest for 5 minutes, or until a bit frothy.

4. Preheat the oven to 170°F. Once the oven is hot, turn it off.

5. Add the applesauce, melted butter, minced onion, onion powder, garlic powder, salt, and 2 cups of flour to the yeast mixture. Using a large wooden spoon, mix for 3 to 4 minutes before adding 2 more cups of flour and mixing for another 2 to 3 minutes. If the dough is quite sticky, add the remaining ½ cup of flour.

6. Transfer the dough to a lightly floured surface and knead for about 5 minutes, or until it forms a soft ball. Lightly grease a large bowl and place the dough in it. Cover with a clean kitchen towel and place in the oven (with the door slightly open) for 30 to 60 minutes, until doubled in size. While the dough is rising, line two large baking sheets with parchment paper and set aside.

7. Once the dough has doubled in size, punch it down, place it on a lightly floured surface, and roll it into a rectangle about ½ inch thick. Use a large biscuit cutter (or a round cookie cutter about 5 inches in diameter) to cut out 16 donuts. Transfer to the prepared baking sheets, cover with a clean kitchen towel, and let rest for 15 minutes.

CONTINUED ▷

8. While the donuts are resting, preheat the oven to 350°F.

9. Bake for 12 to 15 minutes, or until puffy and lightly golden on top. Let cool completely.

10. **To make the cream cheese topping:** While the donuts are cooling, in a small bowl, combine the cream cheese and everything bagel seasoning.

11. Once the donuts have cooled, scoop out a well in the top of each donut to the center, about 3 inches in diameter, and spoon the caramelized onion filling into the hole. Spread about 2 tablespoons of the cream cheese topping on top of each donut and sprinkle with extra bagel seasoning (if desired).

PER DONUT: Calories: 275; Total fat: 13g; Saturated fat: 3g; Cholesterol: 0g; Sodium: 122mg; Carbohydrates: 35g; Fiber: 2g; Sugar: 6g; Protein: 6g

SUN-DRIED TOMATO AND BASIL DONUTS

PREP TIME: 15 minutes • COOK TIME: 10 minutes

REFINED-SUGAR-FREE

MAKES 6 DONUTS

I love the combination of sun-dried tomatoes and basil. I typically use this flavor pairing for scones or quick breads, but I was inspired one day to see whether it would work in a donut. I've chosen whole-wheat flour for this recipe, because it's not meant to be sweet, but if you want to lighten it up a bit, try using light spelt or all-purpose flour instead.

Vegan butter or nonstick cooking spray, for greasing the pan

1¾ cups (198 grams) whole-wheat flour

¼ cup (36 grams) nutritional yeast

1 teaspoon baking powder

½ teaspoon onion powder

½ teaspoon garlic powder

½ teaspoon kosher salt

¾ cup unsweetened nondairy milk

½ cup sun-dried tomatoes, packed in oil, drained, and chopped

2 tablespoons olive oil

7 or 8 fresh basil leaves, rolled and sliced into ribbons

1. Preheat the oven to 350°F. Lightly grease 1 (6-cavity) donut pan and set aside.

2. In a large bowl, combine the flour, nutritional yeast, baking powder, onion powder, garlic powder, and salt. Add the milk, sun-dried tomatoes, olive oil, and basil and mix well to combine. Using your hands, knead the dough in the bowl to bring it all together.

3. Divide the dough evenly into the pan, filling each well three-quarters full.

4. Bake for 10 minutes, or until a cake tester inserted into the center comes out clean. Cool in the pan for 10 minutes before transferring to a wire rack to cool completely.

PER DONUT: Calories: 183; Total fat: 6g; Saturated fat: 1g; Cholesterol: 0g; Sodium: 184mg; Carbohydrates: 29g; Fiber: 5g; Sugar: 3g; Protein: 6g

CRANBERRY STUFFING DONUTS

PREP TIME: 25 minutes • **COOK TIME:** 30 minutes

REFINED-SUGAR-FREE

MAKES 12 DONUTS

My favorite part of Thanksgiving is always the stuffing. I made these donuts one year to use up leftovers, but then I realized I didn't need to limit them to a holiday treat. This recipe is based on a fresh batch of stuffing, but you could easily use up leftovers, too.

Vegan butter or nonstick cooking spray, for greasing the pans
1 large loaf day-old round sourdough bread, cubed
1 cup unsweetened dried cranberries
3 tablespoons grapeseed oil
2 medium apples, finely chopped
2 medium onions, finely chopped
2 celery stalks, diced

3 fresh sage leaves, chopped
1 small rosemary sprig, stem discarded and leaves finely chopped
3 thyme sprigs, stems discarded and leaves reserved
½ teaspoon kosher salt
½ teaspoon freshly ground black pepper
2 cups low-sodium vegetable broth

1. Preheat the oven to 350°F. Generously grease with butter or spray with cooking spray 2 (6-cavity) donut pans and set aside.

2. Place the bread cubes and cranberries in a large bowl and set aside.

3. In a large skillet, heat the grapeseed oil over medium heat. Add the apples, onions, and celery and cook for about 8 minutes, or until soft and fragrant. Add the sage, rosemary, thyme, salt, and pepper and cook for 1 additional minute.

4. Transfer the mixture to the bread bowl and add the vegetable broth. Stir until well combined.

5. Divide the stuffing mix evenly among all cavities in the prepared pans, packing it firmly into each well.

6. Bake for about 20 minutes, or until the edges are dark brown and the donuts are firm. Cool in the pan for 15 minutes, then transfer to a wire rack to continue cooling.

INGREDIENT TIP: If your bread isn't a day old or stale enough for stuffing, cut it into cubes and leave it out at room temperature overnight, or spread the cubes onto a baking sheet in an even layer and bake at 200°F for 20 minutes.

PER DONUT: Calories: 141; Total fat: 3g; Saturated fat: 0g; Cholesterol: 0g; Sodium: 210mg; Carbohydrates: 25g; Fiber: 2g; Sugar: 9g; Protein: 3g

BLACK OLIVE AND JALAPEÑO DONUTS

PREP TIME: 15 minutes • **COOK TIME:** 15 minutes
REFINED-SUGAR-FREE
MAKES 6 DONUTS

There's this bakery near me that makes the most incredible spicy black olive ciabatta buns. During the pandemic, they were closed for an extended period of time, so I had to resort to making my own. I'm not a huge bread maker, so I decided to try turning them into savory donuts instead.

Vegan butter or nonstick cooking
  spray, for greasing the pan
1 cup (113 grams) whole-wheat flour
1 cup (120 grams) all-purpose flour
¼ cup (36 grams) nutritional yeast
1 teaspoon baking powder
½ teaspoon onion powder

½ teaspoon kosher salt
¾ cup unsweetened nondairy milk
½ cup pitted black olives, chopped
¼ cup pickled jalapeños, diced,
  plus 1 tablespoon liquid from the jar
2 tablespoons olive oil

1. Preheat the oven to 350°F. Lightly grease with butter or spray with cooking spray 1 (6-cavity) donut pan and set aside.

2. In a large bowl, combine the whole-wheat flour, all-purpose flour, nutritional yeast, baking powder, onion powder, and salt. Add the milk, black olives, diced jalapeños and reserved liquid, and olive oil and mix well to combine.

3. Divide the dough evenly into the pan, filling each well three-quarters full.

4. Bake for 13 minutes, or until a cake tester inserted into the center comes out clean. Cool in the pan for 10 minutes, then transfer to a wire rack to cool completely.

PER DONUT: Calories: 208; Total fat: 7g; Saturated fat: 1g; Cholesterol: 0g; Sodium: 255mg; Carbohydrates: 33g; Fiber: 3g; Sugar: 1g; Protein: 6g

SAVORY "CHEESE" AND HERB DONUTS

PREP TIME: 10 minutes • COOK TIME: 30 minutes
REFINED-SUGAR-FREE
MAKES 12 DONUTS / 36 MINI DONUTS

These herb-infused savory vegan cheese "quick bread–style" donuts are delicious as a snack or served with a salad for a light lunch. Vegan sour cream is the key to adding that rich flavor and texture, but if you're looking to make these lighter, swap it out for unsweetened soy-based yogurt instead.

Vegan butter or nonstick cooking spray, for greasing the pans
2 cups (240 grams) all-purpose flour
1½ teaspoons baking powder
1 teaspoon baking soda
1 teaspoon dried dill
½ teaspoon kosher salt
½ teaspoon dried oregano
½ teaspoon dried basil

½ teaspoon dried thyme
1 scallion, both white and green parts, diced
1¼ cups unsweetened nondairy milk
8 tablespoons (1 stick) vegan butter, melted
¼ cup vegan sour cream
1 cup shredded vegan Cheddar cheese

1. Preheat the oven to 375°F. Lightly grease 2 (6-cavity) donut pans or 3 (12-cavity) mini donut pans and set aside.

2. In a large mixing bowl, whisk together the flour, baking powder, baking soda, dill, salt, oregano, basil, thyme, and scallion. Pour in the milk, melted butter, and sour cream and mix until just combined. Gently fold in the shredded cheese.

3. Spoon the batter into the prepared pans, filling each well two-thirds full.

4. Bake for 25 to 30 minutes (18 to 20 minutes for mini donuts, 7 to 8 minutes for donut makers), until a cake tester inserted into the center comes out clean. Cool in the pan for 10 minutes, then transfer to a wire rack to cool completely.

PER FULL-SIZE DONUT: Calories: 199; Total fat: 12g; Saturated fat: 3g; Cholesterol: 0g; Sodium: 282mg; Carbohydrates: 18g; Fiber: 1g; Sugar: 1g; Protein: 5g

CORNBREAD QUESO DONUTS

PREP TIME: 15 minutes • **COOK TIME:** 20 minutes
MAKES 12 DONUTS / 36 MINI DONUTS

Cornbread is an absolute favorite in my house. One day, I decided to switch things up and make my "easy cheesy vegan cornbread" in donut pans instead of a regular baking dish. My kids thought it was the best thing ever and now ask for cornbread donuts all the time.

3 tablespoons warm water
2 tablespoons ground flaxseed
Vegan butter or nonstick cooking
 spray, for greasing the pans
1 cup (156 grams) yellow cornmeal
1 cup (120 grams) all-purpose flour
½ cup (100 grams) granulated sugar
1 tablespoon baking powder
1 teaspoon baking soda

½ teaspoon kosher salt
1½ cups grated vegan Cheddar cheese
1 cup unsweetened nondairy milk
⅓ cup vegetable oil
2 tablespoons agave syrup
½ large red bell pepper, diced
½ large green bell pepper, diced
1 or 2 jalapeño peppers, seeded
 and diced

1. In a small bowl, mix the warm water and flaxseed and let stand for 3 minutes to thicken.

2. While the flaxseed mixture is resting, preheat the oven to 400°F. Lightly grease with butter or spray with cooking spray 2 (6-cavity) donut pans or 3 (12-cavity) mini donut pans and set aside.

3. In a large bowl, whisk the cornmeal, flour, sugar, baking powder, baking soda, and salt. Add the flaxseed mixture, cheese, milk, vegetable oil, agave syrup, red bell pepper, green bell pepper, and jalapeño pepper. Stir well to combine.

4. Scoop the batter into the prepared pans, filling each well about two-thirds full.

5. Bake for 14 to 16 minutes (8 to 10 minutes for mini donuts, 7 to 8 minutes for donut makers), until a cake tester inserted into the center comes out clean. Cool in the pan for 15 minutes, then use an offset spatula to gently move the donuts out of the pan and onto a wire rack to cool completely.

INGREDIENT TIP: Jalapeño peppers add wonderful flavor and mild heat to these donuts. **TO KEEP THESE DONUTS ON THE MILDER SIDE,** discard the white veins or pith from the inside of the pepper, along with the seeds, and only dice the green fleshy part of the pepper.

PER FULL-SIZE DONUT: Calories: 240; Total fat: 12g; Saturated fat: 1g; Cholesterol: 0g; Sodium: 354mg; Carbohydrates: 29g; Fiber: 2g; Sugar: 12g; Protein: 6g

SCALLION AND SMOKED "GOUDA" DONUTS

PREP TIME: 15 minutes • **COOK TIME:** 15 minutes
LOW REFINED SUGAR
MAKES 10 DONUTS / 30 MINI DONUTS

Wanting to shake up a family brunch one weekend, I served these scallion and smoked Gouda cheese "donuts" instead of bagels—and they were an instant hit with everyone. My mother-in-law particularly liked them, because they were "lighter than bagels so she could eat more than one!"

2 tablespoons hot water
1 tablespoon ground flaxseed
Vegan butter or nonstick cooking spray, for greasing the pans
1¼ cups (150 grams) light spelt flour
1 tablespoon granulated sugar
1 teaspoon baking powder
1 teaspoon onion powder
½ teaspoon baking soda
½ teaspoon garlic powder

½ teaspoon kosher salt
½ teaspoon freshly ground black pepper
1 cup unsweetened nondairy milk
3 scallions, both white and green parts, diced
1¼ cups shredded vegan Gouda cheese (I prefer Daiya Smoked Gouda)

1. In a small bowl, combine the hot water and flaxseed and let stand for 5 minutes.

2. While the flaxseed mixture is resting, preheat the oven to 350°F. Lightly grease 2 (6-cavity) donut pans or 3 (12-cavity) mini donut pans and set aside.

3. In a large bowl, combine the flour, sugar, baking powder, onion powder, baking soda, garlic powder, salt, and pepper. Add the flaxseed mixture and milk and stir until just combined. Gently fold in the scallions.

4. Spoon the batter into the prepared pans, filling each well three-quarters full. Sprinkle the Gouda over the donuts.

5. Bake for 12 to 15 minutes (8 to 10 minutes for mini donuts, 7 to 8 minutes for donut makers), until a cake tester inserted into the center comes out clean. Cool in the pan for 10 minutes, then transfer to a wire rack to cool completely.

PER FULL-SIZE DONUT: Calories: 130; Total fat: 5g; Saturated fat: 1g; Cholesterol: 0g; Sodium: 265mg; Carbohydrates: 15g; Fiber: 1g; Sugar: 2g; Protein: 6g

Beignets with Chocolate Dipping Sauce, page 120

CHAPTER 6

NOT QUITE DONUTS

Chocolate Éclairs **116**

Vanilla-Caramel Donut Holes **118**

Cinnamon-Sugar Donut Holes **119**

Beignets with Chocolate Dipping Sauce **120**

Apple Fritters **122**

Raspberry Twists **124**

Walnut Crunch Fritters **126**

Apricot Rugelach **128**

Lamington Donut Holes **130**

Strawberry Shortcake Donut Stacks **132**

CHOCOLATE ÉCLAIRS

PREP TIME: 30 minutes • **COOK TIME:** 45 minutes
LOW REFINED SUGAR
MAKES 6 ÉCLAIRS OR 20 CREAM PUFFS

Get ready to have your mind blown. We're making completely eggless vegan choux pastry—and it's honestly easier than you think! I like custard in my éclairs, but if you're looking to save time, you could substitute your favorite store-bought vegan whipped cream instead.

FOR THE CUSTARD FILLING

1 cup unsweetened cashew milk
1 cup full-fat coconut milk
½ cup maple syrup

¼ cup cornstarch
1 tablespoon vanilla extract
⅛ teaspoon ground turmeric (for color)

FOR THE CHOUX PASTRY

1 cup (120 grams) all-purpose flour
½ teaspoon baking powder
⅛ teaspoon salt
1 cup unsweetened nondairy milk
3 tablespoons vegan butter, at room temperature

1 tablespoon granulated sugar
¼ cup water
2 tablespoons powdered egg replacer
  (I prefer Bob's Red Mill)

FOR THE CHOCOLATE GLAZE

½ cup dairy-free chocolate chips

¼ cup unsweetened nondairy milk

1. **To make the custard filling:** In a medium saucepan, combine the cashew milk, coconut milk, maple syrup, cornstarch, vanilla, and turmeric over medium heat. Simmer, whisking constantly, for 6 to 9 minutes, until thickened. Remove from the heat and let cool completely. Once the filling has cooled, transfer it to a pastry bag fitted with a round tip and refrigerate until needed.

2. **To make the choux pastry:** Preheat the oven to 375°F and line two standard baking sheets with parchment paper, lightly brushed with water. Set aside.

3. In a large bowl, combine the flour, baking powder, and salt. Set aside.

4. In a heavy-bottomed pan, heat the milk, butter, and sugar over medium heat until the butter has melted. Remove the pan from the stove (leave the stove on) and add the flour mixture, mixing well with a spatula until lump-free. Return the pan to the stove and cook over low heat for up to 1 minute, or until the dough forms a ball that comes away from the sides of the pan easily. Transfer the dough to a stand mixer fitted with the paddle attachment or to a large bowl and set aside.

5. In a small bowl, combine the water and egg replacer. Add it to the dough and use a hand mixer (or stand mixer) to work it into the dough, mixing for 30 seconds to 1 minute. Transfer the dough to a pastry bag fitted with a large round tip and pipe the dough onto the lined baking sheets in 3-inch-long by 1-inch-high strips. Be sure to leave a few inches in between each strip of piped dough. Dip your fingers in water and smooth out any edges or peaks left from the piping bag.

6. Bake at 375°F for 20 minutes, then reduce the temperature to 350°F and bake for an additional 10 minutes, or until golden. Let cool completely.

7. **To make the chocolate glaze:** While the éclairs are cooling, in a microwave-safe bowl, combine the chocolate chips and milk. Place the bowl in the microwave and cook in 30-second increments (to a maximum of 1 minute) until melted and smooth.

8. Once the éclairs have cooled, slice each one in half horizontally and pipe the custard onto the bottom half. Dip the top of the top half into the melted chocolate and place on top of the custard.

VARIATION TIP: Pipe the choux pastry into 1-inch rounds to make cream puffs instead of eclairs. Decrease your bake time by a few minutes for cream puffs.

PER ÉCLAIR: Calories: 403; Total fat: 19g; Saturated fat: 11g; Cholesterol: 0g; Sodium: 147mg; Carbohydrates: 52g; Fiber: 2g; Sugar: 26g; Protein: 7g

VANILLA-CARAMEL DONUT HOLES

PREP TIME: 10 minutes, plus 20 minutes to freeze
GLUTEN-FREE, LOW REFINED SUGAR
MAKES 12 DONUT HOLES

If you're watching your refined sugar intake but still want something sweet, these blissful little donut holes are an amazing treat. They're also no-bake, so they don't require heating up a stove. You will need a food processor or a high-powered blender for this recipe.

FOR THE DONUT HOLES

⅔ cup rolled oats
⅔ cup raw cashews
⅔ cup pitted Medjool dates

½ teaspoon vanilla extract
⅛ teaspoon kosher salt

FOR THE GLAZE

¾ cup (85 grams) powdered sugar
2 tablespoons unsweetened
  nondairy milk

½ teaspoon vanilla extract

1. **To make the donut holes:** Line a standard sheet pan with parchment or wax paper and set aside.

2. In a food processor or high-powered blender, combine the oats, cashews, dates, vanilla, and salt and process into a thick dough. If the dough is a bit crumbly, add 1 to 2 tablespoons of water. Roll about 2 tablespoons of dough into a ball and place on the prepared baking sheets. Repeat with the remaining dough. Freeze for 20 minutes, or until firm.

3. **To make the glaze:** While the donut holes are firming up, in a small bowl, combine the powdered sugar, milk, and vanilla and whisk until smooth. Drop the donut holes into the glaze, one or two at a time, and gently scoop out with a fork, letting the excess glaze drip off. Return the donut holes to the parchment-lined baking sheet and let the glaze set.

PER DONUT HOLE: Calories: 117; Total fat: 4g; Saturated fat: 1g; Cholesterol: 0g; Sodium: 28mg; Carbohydrates: 19g; Fiber: 1g; Sugar: 12g; Protein: 3g

CINNAMON-SUGAR DONUT HOLES

PREP TIME: 10 minutes • COOK TIME: 25 minutes

GLUTEN-FREE

MAKES 48 DONUT HOLES

Donut holes are such a fun treat—and there's nothing more classic than a cinnamon-sugar donut hole. I use two 24-cavity donut hole pans for these, but you can use a 48-cavity mini muffin tin instead.

FOR THE DONUT HOLES

Vegan butter or nonstick cooking spray, for greasing the pan

2 cups (240 grams) gluten-free all-purpose 1:1 flour

1¼ cups unsweetened nondairy milk

½ cup (100 grams) coconut sugar

4 tablespoons (½ stick) vegan butter, melted

1½ teaspoons baking powder

1 teaspoon baking soda

1 teaspoon vanilla extract

FOR THE TOPPING

½ cup granulated sugar

1 teaspoon ground cinnamon

1. **To make the donut holes:** Preheat the oven to 350°F. Lightly grease 2 donut hole pans (or a mini muffin tin) and set aside.

2. In a large bowl, combine the flour, milk, coconut sugar, melted butter, baking powder, baking soda, and vanilla, stirring until just combined.

3. Spoon the batter into the pan, filling each well about ¾ full.

4. Bake for 20 to 25 minutes, until a cake tester inserted into the center comes out clean. Cool in the pan for 10 minutes, then transfer to a wire rack to continue cooling.

5. **To make the topping:** In a small bowl, combine the sugar and cinnamon. Roll each donut in the cinnamon-sugar mix and enjoy!

PER DONUT HOLE: Calories: 51; Total fat: 1g; Saturated fat: 0g; Cholesterol: 0g; Sodium: 41mg; Carbohydrates: 10g; Fiber: 0g; Sugar: 4g; Protein: 1g

BEIGNETS WITH CHOCOLATE DIPPING SAUCE

PREP TIME: 30 minutes, plus 1 hour 30 minutes for the dough to rise
COOK TIME: 15 minutes
MAKES 24 BEIGNETS

Get ready to party like it's Mardi Gras with these easy, baked beignets dusted in powdered sugar and dipped in a deliciously rich chocolate sauce. Beignet (pronounced ben-YAY) is the French word for "fritter," and they are a legendary treat in New Orleans, which leans heavily on French influences and culture.

FOR THE BEIGNETS

1¼ cups unsweetened nondairy milk
¼ cup (50 grams) coconut sugar
1 (¼-ounce) packet active dry yeast
½ cup unsweetened applesauce, at room temperature
¼ cup coconut oil, melted
1 teaspoon vanilla extract
1 teaspoon grated lemon zest
¼ teaspoon ground nutmeg
4½ cups (540 grams) all-purpose flour

FOR THE CHOCOLATE DIPPING SAUCE

⅓ cup (28 grams) dark cocoa powder
¼ cup (50 grams) granulated sugar
¾ cup unsweetened nondairy milk
⅓ cup (60 grams) chopped dark chocolate
⅓ cup powdered sugar, for dusting

1. **To make the beignets:** In a microwave-safe bowl, microwave the milk for 1 minute, or until steaming but not scalding or boiling. Transfer to a large bowl, add the coconut sugar and yeast, and stir to combine. Let it rest for 5 minutes, or until a bit frothy.

2. Preheat the oven to 170°F. Once the oven is hot, turn it off.

3. Add the applesauce, coconut oil, vanilla, lemon zest, nutmeg, and 2 cups of flour to the yeast mixture. Using a large wooden spoon, mix for 3 to 4 minutes before adding 2 more cups of flour and mixing for another 2 to 3 minutes. If the dough is quite sticky, add the remaining ½ cup of flour.

4. Transfer the dough to a lightly floured surface and knead for about 5 minutes, or until it forms a soft ball. Lightly grease a large bowl and place the dough in it. Cover with a clean kitchen towel and place in the oven (with the door slightly open) for 30 to 60 minutes, until doubled in size. While the dough is rising, line two large baking sheets with parchment paper and set aside.

5. Once the dough has doubled in size, punch it down, place it on a lightly floured surface, and roll it into a rectangle about ½ inch thick. Use a pizza cutter or sharp knife to cut the dough into 24 squares. Transfer the beignets to the prepared baking sheets, cover with a clean kitchen towel, and let rest for 30 minutes.

6. While the beignets are resting, preheat the oven to 350°F.

7. Bake for 12 to 15 minutes, or until puffy and lightly golden on top.

8. **To make the chocolate dipping sauce:** While the beignets are baking, in a small saucepan, sift together the cocoa powder and granulated sugar over low heat. Slowly whisk in the milk, stirring constantly, and cook for 5 minutes. Remove from the heat and add the chopped chocolate, stirring until the chocolate is melted.

9. Dust the hot beignets with the powdered sugar and serve the chocolate sauce for dipping.

PER BEIGNET: Calories: 153; Total fat: 4g; Saturated fat: 3g; Cholesterol: 0g; Sodium: 11mg; Carbohydrates: 27g; Fiber: 1g; Sugar: 8g; Protein: 4g

APPLE FRITTERS

PREP TIME: 15 minutes • **COOK TIME:** 25 minutes
GLUTEN-FREE OPTION
MAKES 8 FRITTERS

Nothing says fall quite like a batch of freshly made apple fritters. There's a large Mennonite community about an hour outside my city that has an incredible year-round market, and whenever we would go in the fall, the highlight of the trip was always a hot apple fritter. I've taken that memory and turned it into a healthier, baked fritter that is also dairy- and egg-free.

FOR THE APPLE FILLING

3 cups peeled and diced apples of your choice (about 4 medium apples)
3 tablespoons vegan butter
3 tablespoons brown sugar

1 teaspoon vanilla extract
1 teaspoon ground cinnamon
½ teaspoon ground nutmeg

FOR THE FRITTERS

½ cup unsweetened nondairy milk
1 tablespoon freshly squeezed lemon juice
1 cup (120 grams) all-purpose flour

2 tablespoons granulated sugar
1 tablespoon baking powder
½ teaspoon baking soda
¼ teaspoon salt

FOR THE GLAZE

3 cups powdered sugar
⅓ cup unsweetened nondairy milk

½ teaspoon vanilla extract

1. **To make the apple filling:** In a large skillet, combine the apples, butter, brown sugar, vanilla, cinnamon, and nutmeg over medium heat and cook for 8 to 10 minutes, until the apples are soft. Remove from the heat and let cool while you make the fritter dough.

2. **To make the fritters:** In a glass measuring cup, combine the milk and lemon juice and let stand for 5 minutes.

3. While the milk mixture is resting, preheat the oven to 400°F and line a large baking sheet with parchment paper.

4. In a large bowl, combine the flour, sugar, baking powder, baking soda, and salt. Slowly pour in the milk mixture and mix until a thick dough forms. You can do this by hand with a wooden spoon or in a stand mixer fitted with the paddle attachment. Gently fold in the cooled cooked apples.

5. Using a large cookie scoop, scoop the dough onto the prepared baking sheet.

6. Bake for 12 to 14 minutes, or until the tops are golden brown. Transfer to a wire rack to cool.

7. **To make the glaze:** While the fritters are cooling, in a medium bowl, whisk the powdered sugar, milk, and vanilla.

8. Dunk each fritter in the glaze and return to the wire rack to set.

VARIATION TIP: You can easily make this recipe gluten-free by swapping out the all-purpose flour for a gluten-free 1:1 baking blend.

PER FRITTER: Calories: 298; Total fat: 5g; Saturated fat: 1g; Cholesterol: 0g; Sodium: 98mg; Carbohydrates: 63g; Fiber: 2g; Sugar: 48g; Protein: 3g

RASPBERRY TWISTS

PREP TIME: 40 minutes • **COOK TIME:** 30 minutes
LOW REFINED SUGAR
MAKES 12 TWISTS

These raspberry twists are like cinnamon buns but with a tart, raspberry swirl—and they're a great dessert to have in your back pocket when you're craving a warm, fresh bun but don't want to wait for yeasted dough to proof and rise. I love the combination of tart raspberry and sweet sugar on these, but you can use any variety of fruit jam. For extra texture, try adding chopped nuts along with the jam.

FOR THE TWISTS
Vegan butter, for the baking dish
2 tablespoons granulated sugar
2 teaspoons ground cinnamon
4½ cups (540 grams) all-purpose flour
2 tablespoons baking powder
1 teaspoon kosher salt

1 cup (2 sticks) vegan butter, cold, cubed
1¼ cups unsweetened nondairy milk
½ cup seedless raspberry jam
2 tablespoons turbinado or other coarse sugar

FOR THE VANILLA GLAZE (OPTIONAL)
1 cup (113 grams) powdered sugar
3 tablespoons unsweetened nondairy milk
2 tablespoons vegan butter, at room temperature

1 teaspoon vanilla extract
1 teaspoon grated lemon zest, plus more for garnish

1. **To make the twists:** Preheat the oven to 400°F. Grease a 9-by-12-inch baking dish or line it with parchment paper and set aside.

2. In a small bowl, combine the granulated sugar and ground cinnamon and set aside.

3. In a large bowl, combine the flour, baking powder, and salt. Add the butter and use a pastry cutter or two knives working in a crisscross motion to cut the butter into the dry ingredients, working until the dough is the texture of small peas. Add the milk and gently bring together using a wooden spoon to create a loose dough.

4. Use your hands to knead the dough together, scraping up any leftover bits in the bowl, until it forms a nice, even ball. Rest the dough for 15 minutes.

5. Lightly flour a clean work surface and roll out the dough to about 9 by 14 inches. Spread the raspberry jam in a thin layer over the dough, right to the edge. Sprinkle the cinnamon-sugar mix evenly over the top.

6. Starting from a long side of the dough, gently and tightly roll up the dough into a log (like a jelly roll), with the seam side down. Cut into 12 even slices and place them in the prepared baking dish, ensuring that they are all touching. Sprinkle with the coarse sugar. Bake for 25 to 30 minutes, until lightly golden brown and puffy. Let cool in the pan for 10 minutes.

7. **To make the vanilla glaze (if using):** In a small bowl, combine the powdered sugar, milk, butter, vanilla, and lemon zest using a whisk or a hand mixer on medium-low speed, until creamy. Spread or pour the glaze over the still-warm raspberry twists. Garnish with additional lemon zest if desired.

PER TWIST: Calories: 368; Total fat: 16g; Saturated fat: 3g; Cholesterol: 0g; Sodium: 301mg; Carbohydrates: 50g; Fiber: 2g; Sugar: 11g; Protein: 6g

WALNUT CRUNCH FRITTERS

PREP TIME: 20 minutes, plus 1 hour to chill the dough • **COOK TIME:** 15 minutes
MAKES 10 FRITTERS

I'm Canadian, and one of the most notably "Canadian" donuts is the Walnut Crunch—made famous by Tim Horton's, which is a Canadian national treasure. Fritters are typically fried, giving them that crunchy outer shell, but since we're being a little more health conscious, I'm baking these and using a powdered sugar glaze to give them that first-bite crunch.

FOR THE FRITTERS

2 tablespoons hot water

1 tablespoon ground flaxseed

2 cups (240 grams) all-purpose flour

½ cup (100 grams) granulated sugar

¼ cup (42 grams) dark cocoa powder

½ teaspoon baking powder

½ teaspoon baking soda

¼ cup plus 2 tablespoons unsweetened plain or vanilla nondairy yogurt

¼ cup unsweetened nondairy milk

¼ cup vegetable oil

½ teaspoon vanilla extract

1 cup (113 grams) chopped walnuts

FOR THE GLAZE

1½ cups (170 grams) powdered sugar

¼ cup water

1. **To make the fritters:** In a small bowl, combine the hot water and flaxseed and let stand for 5 minutes to thicken.

2. While the flaxseed mixture is resting, preheat the oven to 375°F and line a large sheet pan with parchment paper.

3. In a large bowl, whisk together the flour, sugar, cocoa powder, baking powder, and baking soda. Add the flaxseed mixture, yogurt, milk, vegetable oil, and vanilla, and using a hand mixer on medium speed, mix until well combined. Gently fold in the chopped walnuts. Cover and chill in the refrigerator for 30 minutes to 1 hour.

4. Place the chilled dough on a lightly floured surface and roll into a rectangle about ½ inch thick. Use a pizza cutter to cut the dough into 10 even pieces. Shape each piece to form a small loaf that is about 3½ by 2½ inches and score it down the middle with a small knife. Place on the prepared baking sheet about 2 inches apart.

5. Bake for 12 to 15 minutes, until set. Cool on the baking sheet for 5 minutes, then transfer to a wire rack to continue cooling.

6. **To make the glaze:** While the fritters are cooling, in a small bowl, whisk together the powdered sugar and water to form a thick but pourable glaze. Brush the still-warm fritters generously with the glaze and return to the wire rack to set.

PER FRITTER: Calories: 333; Total fat: 14g; Saturated fat: 1g; Cholesterol: 0g; Sodium: 89mg; Carbohydrates: 49g; Fiber: 2g; Sugar: 25g; Protein: 5g

APRICOT RUGELACH

PREP TIME: 45 minutes, plus 1 hour 30 minutes to chill • COOK TIME: 35 minutes
MAKES 48 PIECES

I grew up in a Jewish household, and rugelach were a staple at our table. Rugelach are small, crescent-shaped pastries made from a cream cheese dough, filled with jam, nuts (or seeds), or chocolate. Traditionally, the dough is homemade, but I've included a tip below for a store-bought hack to help you make these treats faster.

FOR THE DOUGH

1 (8-ounce) package plain vegan coconut- or soy-based cream cheese

1 cup (2 sticks) vegan butter, at room temperature

¼ cup (50 grams) granulated sugar

1 teaspoon vanilla extract

2½ cups (300 grams) all-purpose flour

FOR THE FILLING

1 cup (114 grams) chopped pecans

½ cup (71 grams) dried currants

½ cup (85 grams) dairy-free chocolate chips

1 teaspoon ground cinnamon

½ cup apricot jam, plus more for glazing

3 tablespoons coarse sugar, for sprinkling

1. **To make the dough:** In a large bowl, using an electric hand mixer on medium-high speed, mix the cream cheese, butter, and sugar for about 4 minutes, or until creamy. Mix in the vanilla.

2. Drop the mixer speed to low and add the flour, ½ cup at a time, until just combined. Transfer the dough to a well-floured surface and roll it into a ball, then cut it into four quarters, shaping each quarter into a disc. Wrap in plastic wrap or cloth and refrigerate for 1 hour.

3. **To make the filling:** In a food processer, combine the pecans, currants, chocolate chips, and cinnamon and pulse until mixed. Transfer to a bowl and set aside.

4. Line two large baking sheets with parchment paper and set aside.

5. Unwrap one disc of dough and place on a well-floured flat surface. Roll out the dough to about a 9-inch round. Using a silicone brush, spread 2 tablespoons of apricot jam evenly over the dough, leaving a ¼-inch border around the edges. (If your jam isn't spreadable, place it in a microwave-safe bowl and warm for 10 to 15 seconds to melt it.) On top of the jam layer, add ½ cup of the nut mixture, pressing it down so that it sticks to the jam.

6. Use a pizza cutter (or sharp knife) to cut the dough into 4 quarters, then cut each quarter into three equal slices—as if you're slicing a pizza. Starting from the wide end of a wedge, roll the dough up toward the pointed end, forming a crescent roll shape. Place on the prepared baking sheet with the thin, pointed edge down and repeat with the remaining dough. Glaze the crescents with additional jam and sprinkle the coarse sugar on top. Refrigerate for 30 minutes.

7. While the rugelach are chilling, preheat the oven to 350°F.

8. Bake for 30 to 35 minutes, until the tops are golden brown. Cool on the baking sheet for 5 minutes, then transfer to a wire rack to cool completely.

VARIATION TIP: You can swap out the homemade dough for store-bought vegan puff pastry. Just thaw it and roll it into a 9-inch-diameter round, then follow the rest of the recipe above.

PER PIECE: Calories: 116; Total fat: 8g; Saturated fat: 2g; Cholesterol: 0g; Sodium: 25mg; Carbohydrates: 11g; Fiber: 1g; Sugar: 5g; Protein: 1g

LAMINGTON DONUT HOLES

PREP TIME: 30 minutes • **COOK TIME:** 15 minutes
MAKES 24 DONUT HOLES

Lamingtons are a classic Australian treat made from sponge cake filled with raspberry jam, coated in chocolate, and rolled in shredded coconut. Since they are already bite-size, I thought it would be fun to turn them into donut holes. If you don't have a donut hole pan, use a mini muffin tin instead.

FOR THE DONUT HOLES

Vegan butter or nonstick cooking spray, for greasing the pan
2 cups (240 grams) all-purpose flour
½ cup (100 grams) granulated sugar
2 teaspoons baking powder
½ teaspoon baking soda

1⅓ cups nondairy milk
¼ cup coconut oil, melted and slightly cooled
1 teaspoon vanilla extract
½ cup seedless raspberry jam

FOR THE CHOCOLATE COATING

1 cup (170 grams) dairy-free chocolate chips
2 tablespoons coconut oil, melted

2 tablespoons unsweetened nondairy milk
1 cup unsweetened shredded coconut

1. **To make the donut holes:** Preheat the oven to 350°F. Lightly grease or spray a donut hole pan or mini muffin tin and set aside.

2. In a large mixing bowl, combine the flour, sugar, baking powder, and baking soda. Pour in the milk, then add the coconut oil and vanilla. Mix with a rubber spatula until just combined, being careful not to overmix.

3. Spoon the batter into a pastry bag or a large resealable bag with a 1-inch hole cut in the corner. Pipe the batter into the prepared pan, filling each well one-third full, then add 1 teaspoon of raspberry jam to each well and cover with more batter until the well is two-thirds full.

4. Bake for 12 to 15 minutes, or until the donut holes spring back when lightly pressed. Cool in the pan for 15 to 20 minutes before removing them.

5. **To make the chocolate coating:** While the donut holes are cooling, place the chocolate chips in a small microwave-safe bowl and microwave in 30-second increments (up to 1 minute total), stirring after each round. Add the coconut oil and milk and whisk until smooth.

6. Place the shredded coconut on a plate or in a shallow bowl.

7. Dip each donut hole in the chocolate, then roll in the coconut and place on a wire rack to set.

PER DONUT HOLE: Calories: 160; Total fat: 7g; Saturated fat: 6g; Cholesterol: 0g; Sodium: 67mg; Carbohydrates: 21g; Fiber: 1g; Sugar: 10g; Protein: 2g

STRAWBERRY SHORTCAKE DONUT STACKS

PREP TIME: 20 minutes, plus 1 hour 15 minutes for the dough to rise
COOK TIME: 15 minutes
LOW REFINED SUGAR
MAKES 16 DONUTS

Strawberry shortcake is a classic summer dessert and one of my personal favorites. Traditionally, I've always made it as a full cake, but I thought it would be fun to try replacing the vanilla sponge with a vanilla yeasted donut. This version lets everyone get their own personal "shortcake," which is good if you're like me and don't want to share!

1¼ cups unsweetened nondairy milk
¼ cup (50 grams) granulated sugar
1 (¼-ounce) packet active dry yeast
½ cup unsweetened applesauce,
  at room temperature
¼ cup coconut oil, melted
1 teaspoon vanilla extract
1 teaspoon grated lemon zest

¼ teaspoon ground nutmeg
4½ cups (540 grams) all-purpose flour
3 cups store-bought vegan whipped
  cream
½ pint strawberries, hulled and sliced
3 tablespoons powdered sugar,
  for dusting

1. In a microwave-safe bowl, microwave the milk for 1 minute, or until steaming but not scalding or boiling. Transfer it to a large bowl, add the sugar and yeast, and stir to combine. Let it rest for 5 minutes, or until a bit frothy.

2. Preheat the oven to 170°F. Once the oven is hot, turn it off.

3. Add the applesauce, coconut oil, vanilla, lemon zest, nutmeg, and 2 cups of flour to the yeast mixture. Using a large wooden spoon, mix for 3 to 4 minutes before adding 2 more cups of flour and mixing for another 2 to 3 minutes. If the dough is quite sticky, add the remaining ½ cup of flour.

4. Transfer the dough to a lightly floured surface and knead for about 5 minutes, or until it forms a soft ball. Lightly grease a large bowl and place the dough in it. Cover with a clean kitchen towel and place in the oven (with the door slightly open) for 30 to 60 minutes, until doubled in size. While the dough is rising, line two large baking sheets with parchment paper and set aside.

5. Once the dough has doubled in size, punch it down, place it on a lightly floured surface, and roll it into a rectangle about ½ inch thick. Use a large biscuit cutter (or a round cookie cutter about 5 inches in diameter) to cut out 16 donuts. Transfer to the prepared baking sheets, cover with a clean kitchen towel, and let rest for 15 minutes.

6. While the donuts are resting, preheat the oven to 350°F.

7. Bake for 12 to 15 minutes, or until puffy and lightly golden on top. Let cool completely.

8. Once the donuts have cooled, cut them in half horizontally spread 2 to 3 tablespoons of the whipped cream on the bottom half of each donut, and top with a few slices of the strawberries. Then place the top half of the donut on top, add a few more strawberries, and dust with the powdered sugar before serving.

VARIATION TIP: Strawberry shortcake is typically made with whipped cream, but if you're feeling ambitious, try filling these stacks with the homemade custard from my Boston Cream Donuts (page 76) and use the whipped cream on top instead.

PER DONUT: Calories: 219; Total fat: 6g; Saturated fat: 5g; Cholesterol: 0g; Sodium: 11mg; Carbohydrates: 35g; Fiber: 1g; Sugar: 7g; Protein: 5g

MEASUREMENT CONVERSIONS

VOLUME EQUIVALENTS	U.S. STANDARD	U.S. STANDARD (OUNCES)	METRIC (APPROXIMATE)
LIQUID	2 tablespoons	1 fl. oz.	30 mL
	¼ cup	2 fl. oz.	60 mL
	½ cup	4 fl. oz.	120 mL
	1 cup	8 fl. oz.	240 mL
	1½ cups	12 fl. oz.	355 mL
	2 cups or 1 pint	16 fl. oz.	475 mL
	4 cups or 1 quart	32 fl. oz.	1 L
	1 gallon	128 fl. oz.	4 L
DRY	⅛ teaspoon	–	0.5 mL
	¼ teaspoon	–	1 mL
	½ teaspoon	–	2 mL
	¾ teaspoon	–	4 mL
	1 teaspoon	–	5 mL
	1 tablespoon	–	15 mL
	¼ cup	–	59 mL
	⅓ cup	–	79 mL
	½ cup	–	118 mL
	⅔ cup	–	156 mL
	¾ cup	–	177 mL
	1 cup	–	235 mL
	2 cups or 1 pint	–	475 mL
	3 cups	–	700 mL
	4 cups or 1 quart	–	1 L
	½ gallon	–	2 L
	1 gallon	–	4 L

OVEN TEMPERATURES

FAHRENHEIT	CELSIUS (APPROXIMATE)
250°F	120°C
300°F	150°C
325°F	165°C
350°F	180°C
375°F	190°C
400°F	200°C
425°F	220°C
450°F	230°C

WEIGHT EQUIVALENTS

U.S. STANDARD	METRIC (APPROXIMATE)
½ ounce	15 g
1 ounce	30 g
2 ounces	60 g
4 ounces	115 g
8 ounces	225 g
12 ounces	340 g
16 ounces or 1 pound	455 g

RESOURCES

AMAZON

Amazon.com

Amazon is a great online destination for kitchen equipment and tools, plus many specialty vegan ingredients. In addition, the Subscribe and Save program can help you save lots of money on your most frequently purchased food items.

KING ARTHUR BAKING

KingArthurBaking.com

King Arthur Baking offers a wide variety of recipes, ideas, and tips for baking both sweet and savory items, along with measurement conversions for weight and volume. Weight measurements for this book were provided by this website.

ONE GREEN PLANET

OneGreenPlanet.org

One Green Planet is your online guide to making conscious and compassionate choices that help people, animals, and the planet. This website contains numerous plant-based recipes and a variety of health information.

TARGET

Target.com

Target offers a wide variety of kitchen equipment and tools both in their physical stores and online. They also carry a decent number of plant-based ingredients.

TRADER JOE'S

TraderJoes.com

Trader Joe's is a neighborhood grocery store with amazing food and drink from around the globe and around the corner. They are a great resource for plant-based ingredients and products.

VEGNEWS

VegNews.com

VegNews is a popular magazine about all things vegan: recipes, travel, product and restaurant reviews, news, lifestyle, and more. Their website provides lots of articles and resources covering a wide range of vegan topics.

WHOLE FOODS

WholeFoodsMarket.com

Whole Foods is a national grocery chain that offers organic and plant-based groceries along with produce and other health-related products.

WILTON

Wilton.com

Wilton is the ultimate online resource and shopping destination for inspiration, recipes, tips, and instructions for bakers and baking.

INDEX

*(Page locators in **bold** indicate a picture)*

A

all-purpose flour, 12
almond flour, 13
apple cider
  Cinnamon and Apple Cider
    Glazed Donuts, 48-49
apple cider vinegar, 30
apples
  Apple Fritters, 122-123
  Caramel Apple Pie Donuts, 90-92
apricot
  Apricot Rugelach, 128-129

B

bacon
  Maple-Coconut-"Bacon"-Glazed
    Donuts, 66-67
baking
  equipment, 7-8, 9
  high-altitude tips, 9
  skills (veganizing), 2
  strategies, 4, 10
  successful, 22
baking powder, 13
baking soda, 13
banana
  Chocolate Chip Banana Bread Donuts, 34-35
  egg substitute, 15, 16
blueberry
  Blueberry Glazed Donuts, 70-71

C

Canadian, 14, 62, 126
Canadian National Exhibition,
  Toronto, 28

caramel
  Caramel Apple Pie Donuts, 90-92
  Coffee-Caramel Nut Crunch Donuts, 56-57
  how to make, 19
  Vanilla-Caramel Donut Holes, 118
chai spice
  Chai Latte Donuts, 26-27
cherry
  Cherry-Glazed D'oh! Nuts, 58-59
  glaze, 58
  juice, 58-59
chocolate
  cake donut, 15, 38, 56
  chocolate chips, 6, 15, 34, 38, 40,
    44, 54, 116, 128, 130
  Chocolate Éclairs, 116-117
  Chocolate Peppermint-Bark-Glazed
    Donuts, 68-69
  Chocolate-Coconut Donuts, 38-39
  Chocolate Chip Banana Bread Donuts, 34-35
  coating, 130
  Coffee-Caramel Nut Crunch Donuts, 56-57
  dipping sauce, 44, 120
  Double Chocolate Frosted Donuts, 54-55
  glaze/frosting, 54, 56, 76, 83, 116
  Spicy Hot Chocolate Donuts, 44-45
  variety of uses, 15
cinnamon, 14, 19, 26, 124, 128
  Caramel Apple Pie Donuts, 90-92
  Churro Donuts, 30-31
  Cinnamon and Apple Cider Glazed
    Donuts, 48-49
  Cinnamon-Sugar Donut Holes, 119
  Gingerbread Donuts, 32-33
  Peach Streusel Donuts, 93-95

coconut
  bacon, 66
  Chocolate-Coconut Donuts, 38–39
  Coconut Custard Donuts, 98–99
  Coconut Key Lime Pie Donuts, 60–61
  cream, 17, 20, 21
  custard, 98
  glaze, 60
  Maple-Coconut-"Bacon"-Glazed
    Donuts, 66–67
  milk, 17
  oil, 6, 18
  shredded, 38, 60, 130
  sugar, 19, 23
coffee
  Coffee Toffee Crunch, 56
  Coffee-Caramel Nut Crunch Donuts, 56–57
  donuts and, 42
  flavoring, 15
  instant, 15, 44, 56
  Vanilla-Glazed Coffee Cake Donuts, 50–51
cranberry
  Cranberry Stuffing Donuts, 106–107
  Winter Cranberry-Orange Donuts, 36–37
curd
  mango curd, 86

D
digital scale, 8
donut
  baking pans, 3, 7–8
  cake-based, 2
  cutter, 8
  cutting, 10
  healthier, 3
  mini donut maker, 8

donut holes
  Cinnamon-Sugar, 119
  Lamington Donut Holes, 130–131
  Vanilla-Caramel Donut Holes, 118
donuts
  troubleshooting tips, 20

E
extracts, 14

F
Filled Donuts, 75
  Blackberry-Basil-Ricotta Donuts, 78–79
  Boston Cream Donuts, 76–77
  Caramel Apple Pie Donuts, 90–92
  Coconut Custard Donuts, 98–99
  Cookies and Cream Donuts, 96–97
  Lemon Meringue Donuts, **74**, 80–82
  Peach Streusel Donuts, 93–95
  Raspberry-mango Donuts, 86–87
  Strawberry jelly Donuts, 88–89
  Stuffed S'Mores Donuts, 83–85
filling
  apple, 122
  buttercream, 96
  caramelized onion, 102
  cream, 11
  custard, 76, 98, 116
  jam/jelly, 14
  lemon curd, 80
  marshmallow fluff, 83
  pastry piping bag, 11
  raspberry cream cheese, 86
  ricotta, 78
  rugelach, 128
flours, 12–13

fritters
  Apple Fritters, 122–123
  Beignets with Chocolate Dipping
    Sauce, 120–121
  Walnut Crunch Fritters, 126–127

G

glaze
  adding flavor, 11, 15, 42
  blackberry, 78
  blueberry, 70
  cherry, 58
  chocolate, 56, 68, 76, 83, 116
  coconut, 60
glaze (*continued*)
  lemon, 64
  maple, 66
  sugar based, 32, 48, 93, 118, 122, 126
  tips for making, 20
  vanilla, 50, 52, 96, 124
Glazed and Frosted Donuts, 47
  Blueberry Glazed Donuts, 70–71
  Cherry-Glazed D'oh! Nuts, 58–59
  Chocolate Peppermint-Bark-
    Glazed Donuts, **46**, 68–69
  Cinnamon and Apple Cider
    Glazed Donuts, 48–49
  Coconut Key Lime Pie Donuts, 60–61
  Coffee-Caramel Nut Crunch Donuts, 56–57
  Donut Shop Glazed Donuts, 52–53
  Double Chocolate Frosted Donuts, 54–55
  Lemon-Poppyseed Glazed Donuts, 64–65
  London Fog Donuts, 62–63
  Maple-Coconut-"Bacon"-Glazed
    Donuts, 66–67
  Vanilla-Glazed Coffee Cake
    Donuts, 50–51
  Zucchini Donuts with Cream
    Cheese Frosting, 72–73
gluten-free all-purpose flours, 13
gluten-free, 13, 23
Granny Smith apples, 90

J

jam/jellies
  blueberry, 70
  raspberry, 86, 124, 130
  strawberry, 88

L

leaveners, 13–14
lemon
  curd, 15, 80
  Lemon Meringue Donuts, 80–82
  Lemon-Poppyseed Glazed
    Donuts, 64–65

M

maple syrup, 14, 19, 23
  Maple-Coconut-"Bacon"-Glazed Donuts, 66–67
Measurement Conversions, 135
measuring cups/spoons, 7
measuring techniques
  dry ingredients, 5–6
  volume/weight, 7
  wet ingredients, 6–7
mise en place, 4
mixing bowls, 7
molasses, 14

N

Not Quite Donuts, 115
  Apple Fritters, 122–123
  Apricot Rugelach, 128–129
  Beignets with Chocolate Dipping
    Sauce, **114**, 120–121
  Chocolate Éclairs, 116–117
  Cinnamon-Sugar Donut holes, 119
  Lamington Donut Holes, 130–131
  Raspberry Twists, 124–125
  Strawberry Shortcake Donut Stacks, 132–133
  Vanilla-Caramel Donut Holes, 118
  Walnut Crunch Fritters, 126–127
nut butter, 15

O

orange
  candied orange peel, 37
  extract, 14
  Winter Cranberry-Orange Donuts, 36–37
  zest, 15
orange curd, 15
oven
  use of, 9

P

pantry space, 4
pastry bags, reusable, 8
peach
  Peach Streusel Donuts, 93–95
Plain and Sugared Donuts, 25
  Chai Latte Donuts, **24**, 26–27
  Chocolate Chip Banana Bread Donuts, 34–35
  Chocolate-Coconut Donuts, 38–39
  Churro Donuts, 30–31
  Gingerbread Donuts, 32–33
  Mocha Sugar Donuts, 42–43
  Salted Pecan Pie Donuts, 40–41
  Spicy Hot Chocolate Donuts, 44–45
  State Fair Mini Donuts, 28–29
  Winter Cranberry-Orange Donuts, 36–37
plant-based alternatives, 2

R

raspberry
  Lamington donut Holes, 130–131
  Raspberry Twists, 124–125
  Raspberry-Mango Donuts, 86–87
Resources, 136–137
rugelach
  Apricot Rugelach, 128–129

S

Savory Donuts, 101
  Black Olive and Jalapeño Donuts, 108
  Caramelized-Onion-Stuffed Everything
    Bagel Donuts, 102–104
  Cornbread Queso donuts, **100**, 110–111
  Cranberry Stuffing Donuts, 106–107
  Savory "Cheese" and Herb Donuts, 109
  Scallion and Smoked "Gouda" Donuts, 112–113
  Sun-Dried Tomato and Basil Donuts, 105
silicone spatulas/whisks, 7
spices, 14
spelt/light spelt flour, 12
strawberry
  Strawberry Jelly Donuts, 88–89
  Strawberry Shortcake Donut Stacks, 132–133
stuffed donuts, 102
sugar, low/no refined, 23

T

Tim Horton's, 126

V

vegan baking
  baking replacements, 12, 17
  is a game changer, 17
  plant based substitutes, 2, 17
  secrets, 21
  tips for success, 22
  troubleshooting, 20

W

whole-wheat flour, 12
workspace
  organizing, 5

Y

yeast, 2, 4
  proofing, 10

Z

zucchini
  Zucchini Donuts with Cream
    Cheese Frosting, 72–73

ACKNOWLEDGMENTS

I am grateful, as always, to the incredible group of people at Callisto Media for bringing this book to life: my editorial team, Vanessa Putt, Anne Goldberg, and Katherine Green; Art and Production for making this book look beautiful; and Sales and Marketing for getting it out into the world.

A big thank you as well to my incredible team of donut testers who baked their way through this manuscript: Laura Davenport, Abby Greenspan, Sheryl Greenspan, Barbi Lazarus, Jonah Pinchuk, and Molly Veale. I couldn't have done this without you!

ABOUT THE AUTHOR

 Ally Lazare is a Toronto-based writer and home cook and baker. This is her sixth published vegan cookbook. Ally has been creating recipes since she was a teen and has spent the last decade developing easy, healthy, and delicious plant-based dishes that everyone can enjoy. When she's not cooking or baking, Ally is busy collecting vintage cookbooks and spending time with her husband and two young daughters.

CPSIA information can be obtained
at www.ICGtesting.com
Printed in the USA
JSHW012232190422
25077JS00002B/6

9 781638 077831